W9-COA-391

FIVE CRAZY NIGHTS

The Survival Guide to
FIVE NIGHTS AT FREDDY'S
and Other Mystery Games

Content packaged by Mojo Media, Inc.
Joe Funk: Editor
Jason Hinman: Creative Director
Contributing Writers: Gerry Walsh, Guthrie Lowe, Barry MacDonald

CONTENTS

INTRODUCTION

For those about to be scared, we salute you!

Welcome to this unique book, where we explore the Five Nights at Freddy's phenomenon. Along the way, we'll help you get the most out of all of the games in the series so far, and even explore the frightening appeal, of scariness.

Indeed, videos showing people getting scared out of their wits while playing the Freddy's series, are as popular as the walkthroughs, which is rare for any game.

What is it that makes us love a jump scare? How do you make something scary for kids, but not too gory? What other games feature survival or jump scare elements that have made the Freddy's games so endearing? Who came up with this clever concept of making the slightly creepy animatronic animals we all see at the local kiddie pizza joint, into menacing denizens of the dark?

We answer all this, and more, in the following pages. So grab this guide and bring it into Freddy's control room with you, and consider it your essential survival handbook for making it through yet one more night at Freddy's.

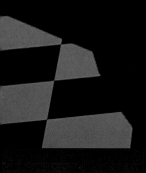

-SORRY!-
OUT OF ORDER

FIVE NIGHTS AT FREDDY'S

You may have been to one of those family restaurants or theme parks that feature crazy characters in costumes entertaining the kids. Chuck E. Cheese's and Walt Disney World come to mind when you're thinking of this kind of thing.

People dressed like teddy bears, party decorations and pizza, the works.

Five Nights at Freddy's is the story of Freddy Fazbear's Pizza, where instead of actually hiring people to walk around in costumes all the time, the owners of the place decided to make the animals robotic so they can walk around and entertain the kids by themselves!

Somehow though, after the restaurant closes and all the customers go home, Freddy Fazbear and his fellow animatronic friends get confused when there aren't any kids running around for them to entertain.

You might think the owners of the restaurant would have paid to have Freddy and his friends looked at, or possibly repaired. But it turns out to be a lot easier on the wallet to just hire a security guard—in this case, you—to watch over them at night and make sure they don't get up to any mischief.

You're in charge of a lot.

You've got your office, you've got your laptop to check in on all of the security cameras placed around the building, and you've got lights and doors on each side of your small office.

Now, we're not going to sugarcoat things—Freddy and his friends can get a bit irrational and most of your job is going to be checking on the security cameras to make sure that they're not getting in any trouble.

Each of the characters has its own spot to spend the night, so if you see through the security cameras that one or more of them have moved, it's time to be on your guard. These animatronic animals are designed to entertain people, and since you're the only person in the building at night, they'll be coming for you.

YOUR TOOLS AND HOW TO USE THEM

When you start the game the first thing you'll notice is your office. It's not very big but there are a couple of important things to pay attention to.

First off is your ability to turn your head—fancy that! When you scroll the mouse back and forth from the left to the right and back again, you'll be able to turn your head in both directions to check the doors on either side of the room.

FIVE CRAZY NIGHTS

Next up are the very obvious buttons you can see on both sides of the room. It'll be pretty easy to figure out what they do but just so you know beforehand, these buttons are for the door and for the lights in the hallway just outside. You're going to want to remember these buttons are there, even on your first night.

Before we look at what you can do by pressing these buttons, let's scroll down to the bottom left of the screen where we can see a couple of very important "gauges".

The first gauge lets you know how much battery power you have left. Like we said before, the owners of this place aren't big on spending a lot of money so you've only got so much power every night.

Once the "Power left" gauge reaches zero, the other buttons for the door, the lights, and even the security cameras will stop working, so you have to be careful how much you use each of those gadgets.

The perfect way to make sure you're being careful is by checking the gauge right below the first one.

Chapter 1: Five Nights at Freddy's

On this gauge, you're actually going to see some colors depending on the buttons you have pressed. The bigger that colored bar gets, as it goes from green to yellow to red, the more power you're using and the faster you're going to drain the battery.

The doors are your last line of defense and will either stay open or shut depending on the press of the button. When you see Freddy or another confused animatronic character just outside your door, you press the button and shut it as fast as you can. Just remember you can't keep them on all night—even keeping the doors closed will drain your battery—so you've got to be careful when you do it. How are you going to see them you may ask? It is night time after all, and things are very dark.

You're going to be able to see them with the lights on, of course, and they work just about the same way as the doors. You press the button to turn them on and press it again to turn the light off, whichever side you're on. Just remember not to keep too much on at a time or you'll lose all of your battery power.

In the middle of your in-game screen you'll see a white rectangle with a couple of arrow symbols in the middle of it. This is what brings up your laptop. On this laptop you're going to see a map of the building and where each of the security cameras are placed throughout.

Altogether there are 11 cameras you can check on throughout the night. It might be hard right off the bat to make sense where everything is placed but try your best. The easiest way to make sense of it all is to start at the little square dot marked "you". If you've been to a mall and looked at one of those map displays they have to show people where all the different stores are, this probably looks familiar.

That little square dot is you, in your office. There are a couple of cameras just outside each door of your office so things are going to get serious if you see Freddy Fazbear or any of his malfunctioning friends hanging around there on either side.

Your last, and possibly the most important tool you've got, is your ears. Yes, you read it right, sounds play an important part in this game.

Whether you've got headphones in or have the

sounds playing from a speaker system, one of the best ways to survive Five Nights at Freddy's is by listening for footsteps coming down the hallway toward your tiny office.

But it's not just footsteps you need to be listening for—there are a couple of different sounds that will let you know what might be happening when you're not looking through the lens of a security camera.

The thing about Freddy Fazbear and his animatronic family is that they're a little camera shy. As soon as they know you're looking at them on any of the security cameras, they freeze. So listening to them move is your best option most of the time if you want to know what they're up to.

Speaking of Freddy and friends...

CHARACTERS

Let's touch on just for a moment the subject of who to watch out for on your night-shift security job. There are four of these characters that switch from their daytime "entertain the kids" mode, to one where they just roam around the restaurant so

they stay loose and limber and none of their robotic parts get rusty from not moving.

FREDDY FAZBEAR: Freddy's the main character and the mascot for "Freddy Fazbear's Pizza." He's the lead singer in the band—which you can tell by the mic in his hand while he's on stage—but he's really just a great big brown huggable bear. He's got a hat, he's got a big toothy smile, and sometimes his eyes glow in the dark when he's coming for you. Only sometimes. Watch out for Freddy making his way toward your office at night.

BONNIE THE BUNNY: Bonnie looks a look like Freddy—he's big and cuddly, but pink and rather than a nice hat on his head he's got a red bowtie and when he's on stage he strums a guitar. He also doesn't have any top teeth or eyebrows. Even though he has a hard time making different expressions, it's not hard to tell what he's thinking as he wanders around at night with the rest of his animatronic bandmates.

CHICA: The third member in the band is Chica—she's a chicken and the backup singer. She's got eyebrows but like Bonnie doesn't have any top teeth. Then again, she's a bird so that kind of makes sense. One thing about her is that she's wearing a big white bib with the words "LET'S EAT" on the front in all capital letters. Chica hangs out in different rooms than the others at night. As you might be able to tell by her bib, they're usually rooms that deal with food, like the kitchen and the dining area.

FOXY: Foxy is a pirate. He's also a fox. When you're looking through the security cameras and you come to a scene with a big purple curtain, you're at Pirate Cove. Now, Foxy is the only animatronic animal who's currently broken down completely at the moment. The big purple curtain is even drawn during the day because Foxy isn't doing any more shows. However, if you ever see Foxy's face peeking through that curtain at night, back out of the security camera screen as quickly as you can and close both the doors. You're only

going to see Foxy's face if he's coming for you, and he moves pretty fast.

GOLDEN FREDDY: There's one last character that you may or may not see during your five nights at Freddy's. He's called Golden Freddy and he's really just a dreamy version of Freddy with no eyes. It's rare to ever see him because there's a certain couple of things that need to happen first before he appears. Because he's so rare, however, if you ever do see him, it's game over. Golden Freddy will get you even if you've got both doors to the office closed. If he gets you, he does it so well that it will close the game altogether, forcing you to restart the whole game if you want to keep playing.

YOUR FIRST FIVE NIGHTS

Your First Night: You'll start with the phone call from the last security guard. Listen to what this guy has to say because he gives a lot of helpful hints as to how to deal with the different animatronic characters wandering around at night. The call will end around 2:00 am, and during the time that he's

talking you should be pretty safe from Freddy and friends wandering around and coming for you. It's your first night after all, so it'll be the easiest.

Take this opportunity to explore your surroundings a little bit. We know there's not a lot to see but at least you can check on the security cameras and get familiar with where they're all located and what each one sees. Don't go too crazy though—remember, you've still got to watch out for your battery power down at the bottom left of the screen.

The three main characters you have to watch out for always start out at the beginning of the night at the "Show Stage" (Cam 1A). During the day this is where Freddy Fazbear, Bonnie the Bunny, and Chica play their instruments and sing songs for the children coming to visit the restaurant. Normally this is where they should stay during the night. So this is the security camera you should be checking the most, as it's going to tell you who's out of place and moving around the building.

For the most part in Five Night's at Freddy's, there are really only about four different cameras

you need to pay attention to the most. There's the Show Stage (Cam 1A), Pirate's Cove (Cam 1C), and the security cameras just outside the doors to the security office (Cam 2B and Cam 4B).

Check the "Show Stage" to see who's missing from the lineup and on-the move, "Pirate's Cove" to see if Foxy is peeking out from behind his curtains, and lastly "W. Hall Corner" and "E. Hall Corner" to see if anyone's hanging right outside your doors.

You can follow Freddy Fazbear and the other animatronic characters as they wander through the other rooms of the restaurant but really it's only going to become your problem if they get too close to you. It's better to just keep an eye on who's missing from the stage and pay attention to who makes it too close to the office.

When you hear someone coming down one of the hallways and you're not completely sure who it is—maybe you missed them on the security camera or you're not checking every area on purpose—here are some good rules to follow depending on who shoes up at your door:

Chapter 1: Five Nights at Freddy's

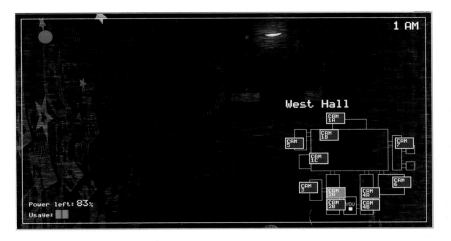

- When Bonnie is coming for you, she'll usually show up at the door on the left.

- If the purple curtains ever open up in Pirate's Cove and Foxy is on his way, then more often than not he's going to show up at the left door as well. (Sidenote: if the curtains are all the way open and Foxy's not behind them, you know he's on his way. Check security camera 2A and you'll see him running toward you. Shut that door!)

- The lead singer Freddy Fazbear comes through the door on right most of the time when he's coming for you. Sometimes, but not very often, he will come through the left.

- Chica comes through the door on the right just like Freddy but this will be the only door that she comes through.

As we mentioned before, one of the most important tools you have to use is your ears—listen for the band members fumbling about in other rooms or wait to hear the footsteps coming down the hallway right outside your doors.

There won't be a lot of stuff happening during your first night—chances are you may not have to use the door-closing button more than once. Keep your guard up though—Freddy, Bonnie, Chica, or even Foxy can still surprise you at random.

A good strategy to use is to wait until you hear footsteps nearby. If you hear them at all, check the "Stage Floor" to see who it is, then quickly scroll through all the rest of the cameras to find out who it is and where they moved to. If you can figure out who's moving around the most, chances are that's going to be the one coming for you.

If you see through the door by using the light switch button that someone's about to come in and get you, close the door! Whoever it turns out to be is going to wait there a few moments before deciding to leave. If you want to check and see if anyone's still outside the door, turn on the light and you'll be able to see the shadow of whoever it is through the window. Other than that, just like when they're coming closer, you're going to

be able to hear footsteps of Fazbear and friends as they walk away.

A good pro tip for when you think you hear someone coming down the hall is to quickly flash the lights on the side you hear the footsteps—chances are you'll catch the whoever it is just before they rush in. It's a good strategy most players of Five Nights at Freddy's use—after all, that's what the lights are there for.

Stay brave and keep checking the right cameras and 6:00 am will roll around before you know it.

Your Second Night: Your second night is a lot like your first, but things are getting serious a little bit quicker than they did the night before. You're going to start hearing footsteps even before the phone call with your old night guard friend is done.

The trick from now on will be to keep an eye on where everybody is. So if you're hearing footsteps, try to locate who is making those sounds as quickly as you can. And check the map when you see Freddy Fazbear or any of his friends so you know where they are.

Keep the list of which character will pop up at

Chapter 1: Five Nights at Freddy's

which door handy while you're checking where all these characters are. Depending on which room you find Freddy, Bonnie, Chica, or even Foxy (he might be running down the hall towards you) in, you might have to worry less or you might have to worry more.

For the most part, though, keep up with the tactics you learned in the first night. Listen for footsteps, check the "Stage Floor" security camera to see who's been moving around, and prepare yourself to close the doors to the office at a moment's notice.

A new tactic you're going to want to get used to is flickering the lights on both sides of the room whenever you hear some footsteps getting closer. Sometimes Freddy Fazbear and his bandmates are sneaky and you might not always catch them on the security camera. You know they are coming for you, so flicking the lights to check is going to be your last chance to be warned someone's at the door. There's always a small window of time where they wait at the door before they pounce, and if you're quick enough you can turn off the light and slam the door fast enough to save yourself.

If you've managed to get the door down in time, and you're still alive, you're still not safe yet. These animatronic animals aren't going to go away just because the door was closed. Freddy and his friends are going to stick around just in case you want to open the doors again to check and see if the coast is clear.

Kind of clever, aren't they?

Well, you're clever too. If the door's open, you can use the light switch to check the area just outside it. But when the doors are shut, you can still turn on the light and just a little ahead you'll be able to see the light through the window into the hallway.

If someone's still waiting outside the door for you open it again, press the light-switch. Instead of just seeing light out in the hallway, whoever is standing in front of the light will cast a shadow, letting you know that either Freddy or one of his friends is still waiting for you.

This rule is different for each side of the room. When you turn on the light with the door shut on the left side, all you're going to see is either the shadow of whoever is blocking the light or just the

regular lit up area where the light normally shines.

If we go over to the right side however, shutting the door and turning on the light will let you see whoever's in the hallway. For example, if Chica happens to show up at the right side of the room you're going to shut the door quickly, of course, but when the door is shut you can turn on the light and you will see her peaking in through the window.

The only one this isn't going to work for is Foxy. As soon as you close the door when Foxy is coming for you, he's gone almost right away, so you don't have to worry about checking with the hallway light. Remember that these guys are clever and sometimes you might shut the door for Foxy but he could be working together with any of the other characters roaming around the restaurant. So even if Foxy gets stopped by the door it might still be a good idea to use the hallway light and check for the shadow. You know when Foxy's gone because he's going to knock on the closed door three times. As soon as he knocks that third time, you're safe from Foxy for now. But that doesn't always mean you're safe from everyone else.

Other than keeping those things in mind, just make sure to keep up with the regular stuff like watching your battery power. A good rule to follow for how much power you have left is to look at the clock and if half the night has ticked by and you're at about 50-70 percent battery power left, then you're managing your different tools well.

As you get further into the game you're going to have to use the security cameras, the lights, and the doors more and more, so getting into the habit of using them smartly is helpful at the beginning of the game.

Your Third Night: The phone call on the third night is a lot less charming than it has been the last two nights, so now you know what's waiting for you if you let in Freddy or one of his animatronic band members. Don't sweat it, though!

There's going to be less information for us to give you as we get into the later nights. All you need to know is that as the game progresses further, things start to happen faster. So you might have noticed by now that after the first night, you can already hear footsteps moving around the building during your phone call. If you check the "Show Stage" security camera, chances are one if not all of the characters are already out of place and in different rooms.

Freddy, Bonnie, Chica, and Foxy are a lot more comfortable with you now and this is just going to keep getting worse the more nights you spend there.

At this point you might see that some of the security cameras are blacking out occasionally, only letting you hear what's going on rather than see anything. From the start of the game, this is the case only for the kitchen.

It's now all the more important to use your ears and listen for different sounds other than the footsteps. Do you hear what sounds like the rattling of dishes? Someone's probably in the kitchen, so you can check the map and see if there's anyone close by that area.

You might even hear Freddy start laughing occasionally. I'm not sure we really need to tell you that's not a good thing. We said before that Freddy shows up most often at the right door and only

sometimes will be at the left door. When Freddy laughs, watch the left door because that's usually what lets you know he's coming and he thinks he's being funny trying to surprise you by showing up at the other door.

Another thing to watch out for now is the hallucinations. You might have seen a couple before, even some on your first night at Freddy's, but now they might be happening more often. Try to keep a cool head because in terms of gameplay they're not going to change much.

Your Fourth Night: Throw out most of what you've learned the three previous nights about the behavior of Freddy Fazbear and all of the other animatronic characters. Starting on the fourth night, things are going to get a lot more serious and the patterns and behaviors you've come to expect from all the characters you've grown to love will change.

That's fine though, because that just means you're going to have to change up how you play.

Foxy and Freddy have both had enough of you at this point and they're both really eager to grab you

Chapter 1: Five Nights at Freddy's

and stuff you into one of the spare character suits.

Foxy in particular is out to get you—he's not just going to go after you but now he'll start trying to do something about how much power you have left to use for the doors, lights, and security cameras. Like you weren't having a hard time worrying about that already!

From now on you're going to want to start paying more attention to Foxy because a good way to get him to slow down and not cause mischief is to keep an eye on his purple curtains at "Pirate's Cove".

When he does bust out, check to see if he's running down the hallway (camera 2A) and close the door. You'll hear him bang on it as usual but now it might be four knocks before he gives up. When he heads back you might even lose a percentage or two of battery power because of Foxy's tampering.

*Foxy bangs on your closed door four times now. You want to save on battery power now more than ever, so a good trick is to open the door when you hear the first knock. The door will open and the

knocks will keep happening but Foxy will already be gone and hiding back behind his curtains. It's a little glitch but all the power you save helps. *

As a rule the other characters are going to take more of a back seat for the last two nights but it's random so you never know who might start working together. When you see all of Freddy Fazbear's bandmates on the security cameras now, you'll notice that they're no longer just standing still. Their heads start to twitch the longer the night goes on.

We covered Foxy—now you know that to keep him in check and react to him well enough is to keep checking on his purple curtains. Freddy, on the other hand, is just going to start laughing more and more on the last two nights.

When Freddy laughs, you have to be on your guard.

Listen to the footsteps in particular when you hear him laughing because while normal footsteps are going to be slow and steady, if Freddy's decided to come for you then you're going to hear fast shuffling steps moving pretty quickly in your direction. If that happens then you need to figure out where he's coming from as quickly as you can

and shut the right door or your goose is cooked.

Other than that just keep your normal guard up for the rest of the characters and conserve your battery power as best you can. If you survive we can move on to the last night.

Your Fifth and Final Night: It's crunch time everybody! By now you've played the game enough to know all the different buttons to press and what everything does, and you've probably got some good strategies ready to use. That's good

because this is the night you're going to need them.

You've been checking security cameras and turning on the lights but now it's time to start zipping through them as fast as you can. Focus only on a couple of different security cameras, and the ones you do use, make sure to only keep them open for a split second—just long enough to check and see if anything's changed—then close it. The less time a security camera or light is on the less power you use up and the better chance you're going to have of surviving the night.

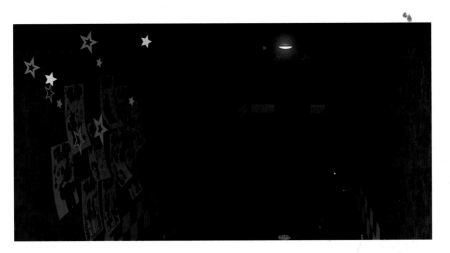

Foxy and Freddy are going to be your main targets and the most active out of all the characters, just like the night before, but now it's even worse.

You've been doing a good job keeping Foxy slow and behind his curtain for the most part by continuing to check up on him pretty often, but now it's time to start doing that for Freddy. Start checking the "Show Stage" security camera and try to keep Freddy from going about his business as much as you can.

Try to use the security cameras just to keep an eye on those two, and for everyone else turn up the volume and listen for any footsteps. If you think you might be about to get jumped by anyone else, then just use the hallway lights to check and see before closing the doors.

It's important now to only check on the other characters when you actually hear something.

It's time to develop a nice and steady rhythm, checking all the things you need to on the security camera about once every 3-4 seconds, then just rinse and repeat until something changes and you've got to act. Don't let any weird noises in other rooms or hallucinations distract you. Just keep up with your routine and you should be able to make it through the final night.

If you can get this strategy down pat you'll be able to survive the fifth night and you might even have some power left over by the time 6:00 am rolls around.

If you managed to make it through the five nights, congratulations! You get your paycheck and you get to go home and find a normal job where you're not risking your life every night in a pizza restaurant. **Or do you?** 🔘

FIVE NIGHTS AT FREDDY'S 2

Welcome back to Freddy Fazbear's Pizza! It's new, it's been redone, and you're going to see right off the bat that you're not back in your rinky-dink little office where you spent all your time in the first game.

Everything has been redone. The whole restaurant has been renovated almost from the ground up and things are better than they ever were before. You've got air vents on either side of your office instead of doors and the power system has been improved, so now you don't have to worry about wasting too much power at night when you're using the security cameras to keep an eye on things.

Be careful, though—just because you've got all the power you need to use the security cameras as much as you want, that doesn't mean you're safe. There's a whole team of new and poorly built animatronic characters prowling around at night looking for restaurant customers to entertain, and you're still the only one there.

The new location for the door to your slightly larger security office is directly in front of you. So if any of the usual crowd of animatronic animals want to come pay a visit, shine the flashlight straight ahead because a lot of the time this is where you're going to see them hiding in the dark.

These new guys have been built a little differently—they've been programmed to recognize faces and have a whole library of different faces stored away to recognize any bad guys who might walk through the restaurant's doors. Unfortunately, they are still malfunctioning and it's going to be up to you to figure out how to survive again for all five nights.

Now in each room you can see into with a security camera you have the option to turn on the flashlight and light up any dark corners where things might be hiding. You're going to see your old pals Freddy Fazbear, Bonnie, and Chica, and even Foxy might still be around somewhere but now in a brand-new setting.

New party rooms for the kids, a new stage where all the characters perform for their audiences, and you've even got some security cameras that will see into the air vents in case something gets stuck in them.

Without further ado, let's take a look at the tools you have at your disposal to help you survive Five Nights at Freddy's, again.

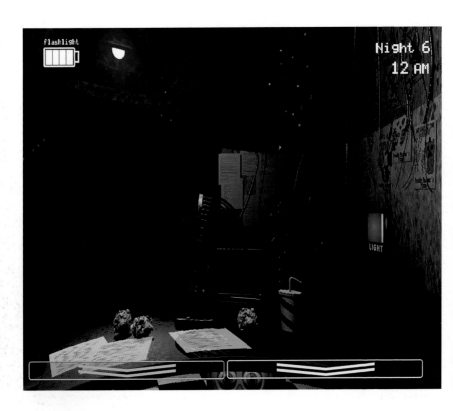

flashlight

Night 6
12 AM

LIGHT

YOUR TOOLS AND HOW TO USE THEM

The Security Cameras & Freddy Fazbear Head:

If you've played the first game you're probably used to using the security cameras to have a look in all of the different rooms around the restaurant. We're in luck because those security cameras are back so if you were comfortable using them before, you're going to have no trouble getting used to these new ones.

If you're on your first night then the playful animatronic animals probably won't be wandering around too much, which means you've got the time to check your new office for a few minutes before things start to get scary.

When you're sitting at your office, take a look at the bottom of the screen. In the first game there was only one little bar you could mouse over that would open up your laptop, but now there are two.

Why are there two, you ask?

Well, it's really close to being the same as it was in the first game. The little bar on the right will bring up the map screen and show you where all of the security cameras throughout Freddy Fazbear's Pizza

are. We'll go over that more in just a sec but for now let's focus on this new second bar that's on the left. You'll notice that it's red and when you mouse over it there is no map screen that comes up.

Introducing your very own Freddy Fazbear head!

That's right, just like the old security guard on the phone at the beginning of the first night will tell you, they remembered that Freddy and all of the other animatronic characters are trying to get you and stuff you into an empty suit. They recognize faces (including yours) so the best way to avoid getting caught by them is to pull up this head and wear it

over your own when someone gets too close. You can keep it on and wear it for as long as you want.

But beware!

This trick isn't always going to work—there are some characters that aren't going to be fooled by the fake head. We'll tell you just who isn't going to fall for the mask in just a little bit.

First let's go back to taking a look at the map and what you can do with all of the security cameras that you couldn't do in the first game.

The rooms you'll see through the security cameras are going to be different because the

FIVE CRAZY NIGHTS

owners of Freddy Fazbear's Pizza spent the money and got a newer, bigger restaurant. So while it's going to be unfamiliar, what you're going to remember is how the map screen actually looks.

Click on the different rectangles to see through the eyes of each particular camera. When you click on a camera you will see into that room and at the top of the map where all the rectangles are it will tell you the name of the room you're looking into.

You'll see a familiar room they've brought back from the first game—the "Show Stage" makes its return so Freddy and friends have a place to play their music for all the children who came to watch. Other than that, there's "Parts & Service," where you can see old broken robots stored to be worked on and fixed at a later date. There's the "Main Hall,", "The Game Area," and "Kids Cove," as well. You can even see a different view of "The Game Area" in "The Prize Corner." There are also four different "Party Rooms" that you might sometimes find Freddy Fazbear and his friends hanging out in.

Lastly, you can check the two different security cameras placed in each of the vents on both sides of your office. You never know what you might see crawling around in there.

Your Flashlight and the Battery

Icon: Let's get out of the map screen and go back to your cozy little office. At the top left of the screen you'll see that there's still a battery icon in this game. Don't worry, it's not there to tell you how much time you have left to use the cameras—like we said earlier, the cameras never die. What this new battery icon does is tell you how long you have left to use your flashlight.

It may not seem like much but your flashlight plays an important role in this game. At the start of your first night you will see that to use your flashlight

you press and hold the left control button on your keyboard. When you test it out for the first time you will see that it works right away by shining a beam of light right down the hallway in front of you.

Keep holding down the shift button as you scroll through all the different security cameras and you'll see that there's a dark spot in every room that your flashlight will light up, and if anyone's hiding in that darkness you'll be able to see them.

The Music Box: Check in on security camera 11 to have a look at the "Prize Corner." You'll see the counter where kids can come up and get prizes for the games they've been playing. The more important thing you're going to see is the little gray box slightly to the left of the map that reads "Wind Up Music Box." Underneath the box you can read, "Click and Hold."

You're going to hear the old security guard on the phone talk about this music box at the beginning of your first night. Remember when we mentioned there are some fun characters who aren't going to be tricked by the Freddy Fazbear head? This music box will keep that secret character calm the whole night as long as it keeps playing.

If you're good about keeping the music box wound up all the time you probably won't ever notice this, but there's going to be a small warning that appears if the winding ever gets too low. What this means is that if you forget or purposefully let the music box wind down without bothering to wind it back up, you'll see a small exclamation point appear in yellow at the bottom of your screen. If you let it go any longer it will go from yellow to red, and if it stays at red too long...well let's just say it's going to mean trouble.

Light Switches and the Time: The last important thing that you will see are going to be the light switches to the left and right of your

office. Sometimes when the animatronic characters get sneaky and try to crawl through the vents to say hello, they're going to make it up into your office. You're not going to get any warning if this happens, either. It will be up to you to check these vents with the light switches to see who may or may not be hiding right in front of you.

The last thing you'll want to pay attention to is the clock at the top right of the screen. It doesn't work like a regular clock, something you're probably used to from playing the first game, and you don't get to see

the minutes. It's only going to update every in-game hour until your night is over at 6:00 am and you're safe. Lastly, you'll be able to see what night you're on just above the clock—night 1 is going to be the easiest and it gets more and more difficult as you progress through each night, making night 5 the most difficult.

Your Ears: That's right, noises make a comeback in this game and just like in the first Five Nights at Freddy's, the things you hear and how you react to hearing them could make or break this game for you.

FIVE CRAZY NIGHTS

There are many more noises and creepy sounds to listen for and be afraid of now. You might even hear some giggling now and then or maybe the voice of a small child saying "Hello."

It won't be such a big deal at the start—the first couple nights are rather tame. Make sure to remember which sound means what early on as the last couple nights are pretty vicious. It gets to a point where you can't check the cameras fast enough and end up having to rely on only your ears to tell you what animatronic character is sneaking around and getting up to mischief.

Like footsteps in the last game, telling you who was coming closer to your office, in this game what you want to listen for is the bumps and thumps in the metal ventilation system. This is going to tell you who's crawling around in there and give you a heads up at who's planning to jump out at you from either side of the room.

THE NEW CHARACTERS

The same animatronic animals you know and love from the last game are still around, but the owners of the restaurant invested in getting some new versions made for the new restaurant.

Now, we won't be going over all of the old characters from the first game—if you've played it you should already know who they are and what they're about. They'll make appearances here and there in this game but the main focus during these five nights should be on the new characters. The new guys will be the ones coming for you so we're going to list them out in the hopes that you will at least recognize who's coming for you.

These new characters are going to seem somewhat familiar—it's not your imagination. What the restaurant owners did was take the characters you already knew and loved and gave them a fresh

new design so they'd be more appealing to the kids. To repeat, however, the old characters are still around, so keep that in mind when you play the game.

Toy Freddy: Our first new character is a spruced up version of the old Freddy Fazbear. This new version is more detailed and the color scheme is a lot better. Like the original Freddy you'll see that Toy Freddy is a bear, he's brown, and he carries a mic in his hand, because even in this game the "Freddy" character is still the lead singer in the band. He's got rosy cheeks, whiskers, a top hat, and now even wears a nice little bowtie on his chest with some buttons below it. Watch out for his eyes—normally they're going to look just like everybody else's but if he makes it all the way into your office, that changes.

Toy Bonnie: Toy Bonnie looks a lot more like a rabbit in this game compared to the first Five Nights at Freddy's. We're sure you'll agree it won't be so easy to mistake him for Freddy anymore. A lot of the improvements are similar to how Freddy was improved himself. Things like the little whisker spots, the bowtie, and the rosy cheeks seem to be a popular change they made when the restaurant owners spent their money. He's also got a guitar just like the original Bonnie did when they were standing on the "Show Stage." In Five Nights at Freddy's 2, however, sometimes you might see Toy Bonnie walking around with it.

He's got a shiny new coat of paint, green eyes, and a buck-toothed grin to strike a happy feeling into the hearts of the audience.

Toy Chica: Out of all the new characters, Toy Chica probably looks the most like the original. She's still got her bib and she's still holding a cupcake just like in the last game. For some reason though you won't always see her beak.

Just like Bonnie she's got a shiny new coat of paint, with blushing cheeks and new eyebrows that let her show expression better than she ever could before.

What you'll notice about the paint jobs is that Freddy is the only one who is not shiny in this game. We can't tell you why that is—it might just be a design choice from the people who rebuilt these new improved versions—but just remember that if you see anyone shiny at all, chances are it's not going to be Freddy.

These first three animatronic characters all start each night on the "Show Stage," so right away when each new night begins if you check camera 9 that's where you'll find Toy Freddy, Toy Bonnie, and Toy Chica. The next set of animatronics are placed in other areas of the restaurant and it will be up to you to find them before they find you.

Mangle: If you remember Foxy from Pirate's Cove in the first game then just know that this new character looks almost nothing like him. Mangle once upon a time might have been a replacement for Foxy, as the original name for it was meant to be

"Toy Foxy," but right now she—and we're not even sure if it is a she—is basically, well, she's mangled. We won't tell you where to find her (it shouldn't be too hard to figure out) but when you see her for the first time you'll see that Mangle is basically a broken animatronic lying in a heap on the floor. Curious to figure out why she's battered and broken? Make it to the third night and you'll find out.

Balloon Boy: There's a first for everything, and Balloon Boy is the first human animatronic ever featured in Freddy Fazbear's Pizza. Of course, that's not going to make much of a difference—this little stinker is definitely out to get you, too.

Just like the others, he's shiny, with rosy cheeks and a glassy stare that creeps you out. He wears a hat with a propeller on it and he's dressed in red and blue stripes. In one hand he's holding a balloon and in the other he's holding a sign that says "Balloons." Go figure.

This little guy likes to crawl through the vents but he's not going to attack you directly—instead what he likes to do is mess with the lights. So if you

let him have his way he'll make it so you won't be able to use the flashlight or the lights in the vents. If you let him get too far this light tampering will be permanent for the night, so you need to keep an eye on him.

He's creepy, he giggles, and he could spell disaster if you let him get too far into the office.

The Puppet: You heard us mention the music box before and on your first night you probably heard the old security guard on the phone tell you that keeping that thing wound up is a really important part of this job.

The Puppet is the reason why.

The only time you're going to see this guy in the game is if you've left the music box off for too long. He's tall—almost as tall as the ceiling—skinny, and almost completely black. His face is a white smiling mask with hollow black eyes and he's got three buttons on his chest.

It almost makes you wonder if he really is part of Freddy Fazbear's Pizza because he really doesn't look like an animatronic character at all. Especially

not a kid-friendly one.

If you left the music box unattended for too long and the Puppet actually leaves the "Prize Corner" then it's game over. Just like Foxy in the last game leaving his curtain at Pirate's Cove, the Puppet will speed right towards you and not even the spare Freddy Fazbear head is going to fool him.

SURVIVING YOUR FIVE NIGHTS AT FREDDY'S, AGAIN

Night One: Your first night starts out just like you would expect from playing Five Nights at Freddy's. It starts out with a phone call from the senior security guard for Freddy Fazbear's Pizza. He's calling just like he always does to give you some warnings about things you're going to see and experience during your stay here. Isn't that nice of him?

As per usual the first night will be slow, so feel free to take some time and check out what all the new different features of your new office are for while you listen to the phone call. It should take a while, the guy has a lot to say.

Right off the bat you'll be able to check every security camera and see where all of the animatronic guys start each night and you can even start to crank the music box as well. The music box will only start to really need cranking when the other security guard's call is done, however, and even that only happens on the first night. When the second night rolls around you have to worry about the music box right away.

Now that the security guard is done his call you'll most likely be aware of all the things you need to worry about, if you didn't already know them before. Keep an eye on things with the security cameras, use your flashlight to peep into dark corners of each of the rooms, and pay attention to the music box to make sure that it stays wound up. Also keep an ear out for those bumps in the vents—it's only the first night but that doesn't mean someone isn't crawling through there looking to find their way towards you. Pay attention to the sounds getting closer or farther away and check on the security cameras if you need to. Most of all, remember how to protect yourself if anybody gets too close. (Hint: the empty Freddy Fazbear head.)

Don't worry so much about your flashlight battery power at this point—if you want to look around at all the areas with some light, you can. It's not as important to save as much power as you can during the first couple of nights.

In terms of how the animatronic characters are going to behave, we won't tell you the path each one takes as they make their way towards you but we will tell you where each one is going to pop up. It's most likely going to be a surprise anyway but we didn't want to give away too much in this book.

Turn to your left and look at the vent—you don't need to turn on the light but just be aware that Toy Chica, the bird, will be coming through this way when she's trying to get to your office. She's not the only one who's going to come through here but for the first night it'll just be her you have to watch out for. Toy Bonnie will be coming through the vent on the opposite side of the room when it's his turn to pop up and scare you, so have that empty Freddy Fazbear head ready!

While these two characters, and possibly others, can come through those vents it doesn't mean that they won't come straight through the doorway in front of you. It's random where they decide to go so every once in a while it wouldn't hurt to back out of the security cameras and flash your light down the hall to see if anyone's there.

There's a particular noise you can listen for. It happens right before whoever is in the vents jumps out at you. It's a low kind of hum, kind of like the noise you might hear out of an old television tube when it first turns on. This is your cue letting you know that someone's about to pounce, so if you're in the middle of winding up the music box or searching through the other security cameras and you hear something like it, rush quickly to put on the empty Fazbear head and save yourself. The noise is accompanied by the lights flickering, so you can watch out for that as well as listening for the weird noise.

If you keep all these things in mind and are good enough about keeping up with them, the first night should be a breeze. Just don't panic and keep a cool head and things should turn out fine as we head into the second night.

Night Two: You're going to hate this, but in the second night things get amped up, a lot.

If you were thinking it was just going to be

slightly more difficult than the first night, think again because the difficulty spikes a lot higher really fast and you've got to be on your toes the whole night long.

A pro tip for players from here on out is to turn up your volume—this helps you hear important noises that will tell you what's happening so you can prepare yourself for whoever might be coming at you. While we call this a pro tip, please realize that while it lets you hear things a lot better, if you mess up and Freddy Fazbear or one of his friends get you, it's going to be louder and it's going to be a lot scarier so dial up that volume at your own risk.

You were willy nilly with your flashnight on the first night and that was fine but now is the time where you have to start watching how much flashlight power you use and to only use it when you really need to. These animatronic characters are going to be coming at you left, right, and center, and it's only through careful planning that you're going to stay alive.

Foxy from the first game makes a reappearance

on the second night and he'll be there for the rest of the game. A good habit to get into doing is to use your flashlight only on the hallway in front of you to keep him at bay.

Mangle is also going to be on the prowl. She can come from anywhere so be prepared if you see her. Whether she's in the vents or down the hallway you have to be prepare for her because she's quick.

You've been listening to the noises before and from the second night onward the most important noises you have to listen for are the footsteps that tell you someone's walking down the hall directly towards your office, and the bumps in the vents that tell you someone's crawling in the vents. Get into the habit of listening to these two things right from the start and you should be golden.

The second night is also the night that Balloon Boy first makes his appearance. You may have noticed that on the first night he stayed in one spot the whole night long and didn't bother anyone. Well, that stops now and where you're going to find him trying to sneak into your office is through the vent on the left side. Listen for the bumps and if you hear some giggling as well that's going to tell you that it's Balloon Boy crawling around in there rather than one of the other animatronic characters.

While the second night does ramp up the difficulty, it's still going to be a lot of the same stuff you experienced on your first night. Yes, the Balloon Boy will be new and you have to watch out for him, Foxy, and even Mangle, but the second night is really all about developing the right habits of how to play that will keep you alive for the nights to come.

Now if you want to look through the different cameras after hearing footsteps or movement of some sort, you really need to do it fast and barely flicker your flashlight in each room before moving on to the next. You've got until 6:00 am (yes, we

know it's about 8-9 minutes, but still) so you have to conserve as much battery power as you can.

Freddy Fazbear himself is now going to start marching around, that is if he didn't already during the first night. But by night two he's definitely on the move and more often than not you're going to see him directly in front of you down that long hallway. He might start off far back but he'll inch his way forward slowly. Keep using your flashlight as you keep an eye and ear out for the other guys but as soon as Freddy gets almost to the doorway to your office quickly put on the empty Freddy head and wait until he's gone. He might come at you right away or he might come at you after a couple of minutes or he might decide to leave you alone altogether, but keeping the mask on is always your safest bet. Just don't forget that the music box is still playing.

One more note about the music box is that if someone's right in your face and about to pounce but you need to wind that music box at least a little, you can. Whatever saves you time or however long you can get away with it before you need to put on the empty Fazbear head, take the time to wind up the music box or else it could be game over.

So to sum up, conserve your flashlight power as best you can. If you hear footsteps check the hallway—Foxy likes to hang out there, so if you see him flicker the flashlight in his face a bunch and he should leave. Foxy can get you even if you're wearing a Fazbear head so it's important to make him leave. If you hear something in the vents quickly check them. Keep that music box wound up, even if it's only a little bit at a time. If you see anyone's face sticking out of the vent in your office, put on the empty Freddy Fazbear head right away and leave it on until they jump out and leave. Listen for the giggles and the "Hi" from Balloon Boy and don't let

him mess around with your lights. Lastly develop good habits for where you're checking and how fast you can do it. The second night is all about learning the patterns that the different characters use when they're moving around the restaurant and using your tools properly to respond to them. Things are only going to get harder as we head into the third night.

Night Three: We're sure you're properly spooked after seeing that video from inside the Freddy Fazbear animatronic. We're not going to tell

you what it means here, it'll be up to you to figure it out before the game is over.

It's starting to get really crazy now so we're going to suggest a few changes to the strategies you learned the night before.

Remember Foxy? When he appears in the hallway the best way to get rid of him is to shine the flashlight in his face. At this point though, if he appears too often you're going to waste too much power trying to get him to go away. If this keeps up you won't have enough to last you until 6:00 am, so

FIVE CRAZY NIGHTS

now what you're going to do is to blink the flashlight at Foxy (if you see him in the hallway) five times for at least half second each. This will still work to send him away and it takes as little amount of flashlight battery power that you can spare to do it.

Secondly, go over to the music box and wind it up, as you're holding down the "wind up" button say "One Mississippi" in your head. Did you do it? That's how long you should hold down the music box "wind up" button from now on, pretty much no more than a second, because you won't have time anymore to wind it up all the way. Every second you spend winding it is a second that someone can creep into your office and get you.

The old Five Nights at Freddy's characters are making their comeback now so you now have to watch out for all of the new guys and all of the old ones. If you happen to see any of the old animatronic characters make it into your office, put on the Freddy Fazbear head right away. You might not recognize them anymore—they're kind of broken and even scarier than they ever were before—but make no mistake these guys are fast and back with a vengeance. If you wait even a second too long it's game over so as soon as you see them that has to be your immediate reaction. This is also the rule whenever you see any of the old characters in the vents. Even if you see the original Bonnie crawling around the vent on the security camera, put on the mask right away. You only have a split second between seeing them and putting the mask on. These guys mean business.

As the night begins, start to practice winding the music box and quickly switching back to the security office. You need to be able to do this really fast from now on and almost every second thing you do should be to go back and wind up that music box, even a little.

Another thing to start doing regularly is to check the security cameras in the vents—there are going to be more and more people popping up in them and the more time you give yourself to prepare for them, the better.

Are you hearing that weird echoing, creepy music that happens every so often? If you do, that usually means someone is in the dark hallway right in front of you. It could be anyone but more often than not it's going to be Foxy. Remember what we said about the flashlight flashes and you should be fine. That music is usually a big indicator that one of the characters is about to do something.

You might notice sometimes that your flashlight won't shine down the hallways when you hold down the button. This is another warning that something's about to happen, so prepare yourself for the worst. Stay calm, your flashlight isn't broken for the rest of the night, and even if it turns out to be Foxy in the hallway again, your flashlight will be working in time to send him away.

The original Freddy Fazbear is back too, and just like Toy Freddy, he'll come at you directly from right down the hallway in front of the security office, so apply the same tactics to him as you did Toy Freddy. Wait until he's really close, then throw on the empty Freddy Fazbear Head and you should be fine.

So now your focus should be on three things— the music box, checking in front of you down the hall, and checking the vents to either side both on the security cameras and actually in your office. If you can check all of these things and respond well enough by continuing to wind up the music box when you can, and using both the flashlight and the empty Fazbear head when you need to, you should be able to make it through the night.

By the end of the night you should be spending most of your time either underneath

the mask or winding up the music box, with only occasional breaks to check down the hallway when you hear that creepy music letting you know that Foxy is on his way.

If you can keep up with all of this then you've made it to the fourth night and you're rewarded with yet another spooky video from inside one of the animatronics!

Night Four: Night four is basically about how skilled you are at this point. A couple of things have changed that make everything you've been doing to stay alive up until this point way harder.

The animatronics are going to start moving around a lot faster, getting up to mischief in the vents and coming right for you directly down the hallway.

Now even the music box is going to be affected, winding down a lot faster than it did before, meaning you're going to have to check up on it a lot more often or else The Puppet is coming for you. Have strength, because there is a way to get through this night despite how hard it seems.

FIVE CRAZY NIGHTS

You're going to be using one strategy all night long. It may seem a little boring to be doing the same thing over and over until 6:00 am but if it keeps you alive then it's probably worth it, wouldn't you say?

This strategy works in just five easy, repeatable steps:

· First, check one of the vents in your office by turning on the vent light. It doesn't matter which vent you check.

· Next up is to look straight down the hallway with your flashlight to see who's there.

· Now you need to check the other vent by clicking on the other light switch. This is going to be different for everybody depending on which vent they checked first. Just know by the end of this routine you need to have checked both vent lights in your office.

· Head over to the music box on the map and wind it up as much as you can before you need

to go back to your office to put on the empty Freddy Fazbear head.

· The last step obviously is to wear the empty Fazbear head for as long as you need to, if you even need to, because it's not guaranteed someone's going to be there waiting for you. Although this late in the game chances are someone will definitely be there waiting for you.

The last thing we're going to mention here is to watch out for Mangle. She's going to be all over the place and a big part of the job is reacting to her as quickly as you can by wearing the Fazbear head. If you don't manage it in time she might sneak into your office and once she's there, she won't leave. Deal with Foxy first with the flashlight but never forget Mangle.

So, that's the strategy—rinse and repeat those steps, listen for audio warnings, and watch out for Foxy and Mangle. Lastly, be as quick as you can when switching from the security cameras to wearing the Fazbear head. As soon as you see someone in your face you need to wear

Chapter 2: Five Nights at Freddy's 2

it. With all of that down you should be able to survive the night.

Night Five: Now that the final short and creepy video is over (along with the creepy message afterwards) we head into our fifth and final night.

Do you remember the strategy you learned to deal with the previous night? You know, the one you read about maybe a couple of seconds ago? That's good because that's the strategy we're going to be using again to get through this night. Turns out it's a pretty good one—here's hoping you got good at it.

This is by far the craziest night. The sounds, the movements, the animatronics creeping around—it's all going to go by super fast now and the only thing standing between you and that sweet morning sunlight is how fast you can react and how well you can stick to the plan you stuck to last night.

One big change you're going to notice if you're in the middle of winding up the music at the wrong time is that now if someone creeps into your office they're going to close the laptop on you so you're staring right into their face. If that happens, don't panic—by now you should be good enough to use

that split-second of time to throw on the empty Freddy Fazbear head to protect yourself from whoever it might be. It's possible to do, so you can definitely do it.

All it takes to beat this night is the same strategy as the fourth night, just much faster, so if you've got talent or practice you should be able to hack it. So with a little luck and a lot of skill you've done it!

Take your check and maybe find some other job to work at in the future! 🕹

FIVE NIGHTS AT FREDDY'S

Welcome back to the third installment of your favorite horror jump-scare video game franchise, Five Nights at Freddy's 3!

If you're playing this game after having gone through and beaten the previous games in the Five Nights at Freddy's series, then prepare for a shock because this game is different in a big way compared to the other two. The Freddy Fazbear's Pizza restaurant is gone and done with. No more party rooms or stages and no more confused animatronics walking around in the night trying to off the only security guard working to try and protect the place. No, things are much different this time around.

The new place you find yourself working is a sideshow attraction based off of the scary things that went down at those old locations. It's hosted in an amusement park, it's one of those "house of horrors" attractions that everybody loves but with a special twist in that all the scary things that go bump in the night are based off of all the scary things you know and love from the first two jobs as a security guard.

Sounds like a lot of fun, doesn't it? Well, the people who run the amusement park thought so,

and what better way to scare people than to use bits and pieces of real events?

After playing the two previous games you're probably thinking this isn't the best idea—the animatronics they had to entertain the kids were dangerous even when you were inside a family friendly restaurant and now they've made a horror attraction? It almost screams disaster, and yet none of the old animatronic characters have followed all of the stuff from the old restaurants. During the first night it's only you and whatever small pieces and parts of the old place the theme park owners managed to dig up for their attraction.

Rest easy when you sit down in your new office. This at least will be a familiar setup to you. You've got your cameras for spying on the different rooms, or anyone going through the spook house who might be hiding in the corner. There's the clock at the top left of your screen and you'll see a big window just to the right of your seat where you can see out into the hallway beyond.

A new feature you might be surprised to use is the audio function on the security cameras. Now whenever you check on a particular room you can

check to see if there's any sound in there playing at the same time. You know, just in case.

It's a walk down memory lane for any old players who've been following along in the series of the Five Nights at Freddy's games, and to anyone who's just picked up this one for the first time they're in for the scariest treat. There's going to be so much different about this game compared to the others you could almost believe that it isn't related to Five Nights at Freddy's games that came before.

We said almost—it won't be long before you start to see things that are probably a little bit too familiar. But before we go into what those things might be let's have a look at what tools you're going to be working with as you once again try to make it through Five Nights at Freddy's.

THE NEW TOOLS AT YOUR DISPOSAL

Your New Office: The first thing you're probably going to notice is just how much bigger this office is compared to your old ones. Because

of this increase in size it's now going to take just a little bit longer to scroll from one side to the other. Just like Five Nights at Freddy's 2, there won't be any doors for you to close but there still is one open doorway on the left.

Scroll around the office and you'll notice some new things, like the big window that shows you the hallway outside and some fancy ceiling lights. You're also going to see a lot of old stuff that will be really familiar, like the metal desk fan, some bits and bobs here and there from the old animatronics,

maybe even an old drawing or two that used to be on the walls in the old restaurants way back when. A crowd favorite are the small stuffed-animal versions of the animatronics that made their debut in the second game.

To the left of your office just before the door you can see there's a nice creepy box full of masks of Freddy Fazbear and friends and what seems to be Toy Bonnie's guitar from a long time ago. Peek just outside your door and you can find what appears to be a hollowed-out shell of some nameless

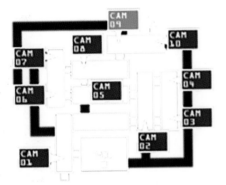

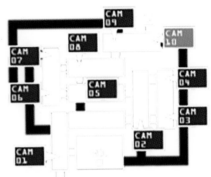

animatronic you might have been scared by before.

All in all, other than what you might sometimes see through that window, there's not much here in the beginning that actually does anything. Heads up, though—just like in the last two games you might be able to find a little Easter egg picture of Freddy Fazbear whose nose squeaks when you click it.

After you've had your fun looking around at all the new stuff, scroll to the far right end of your office and we'll take a look at our new upgraded security camera system.

The New 3 in 1 Security Cameras: On

the far right of the office, you'll see near the top of the screen a blue see-through rectangle with two triangles inside it. Click this to bring up your new and improved system for spying in on different rooms throughout the attraction.

There might be a little bit more static than there used to be in the old cameras but these things weren't built brand-new just for this amusement park. Just like everything else in this horror attraction they tried to make things as real as

they could, and that means going out to get the real security cameras and the real parts and masks from the old restaurants.

Even though the view isn't always the clearest, there's a lot more you can do with this new security camera system than you're probably used to, so let's have a look.

The layout is pretty similar to what you've seen before—click on the different "Cam" buttons to look through the lens of each security camera in each room. It won't be obvious right away but there are some things you're going to actually be looking for.

If you remember Five Nights at Freddy's 2, then you remember there was a ventilation system that some of the animatronics could crawl around in and use to sneak up on you. Well, the airs vents are back and there's a lot more of them this time, so naturally there are a lot more cameras to keep an eye on them all.

Over to the left of the actual map you will see one or two buttons out on their own. We say "one or two" because sometimes you might see one and sometimes you might see them both, but

there's always going to be one of them there and that particular button is the one we're looking at right now. The button on the bottom labeled "Map Toggle" changes the map screen just a little bit. It changes from showing you the locations in all the different rooms you can find security cameras in to just showing you the highlighted area where all of the vents are located and where you can find the different cameras hidden in these vents. You use this "Map Toggle" button to switch between the vent cameras and the cameras in each room.

It's kind of a big change because now you're got two sets of cameras to look through and be aware of as the night goes on.

When you actually click this "Map Toggle" button and you change the map screen, there are a couple of other things you may have noticed. First of all, what are all of those green horizontal lines you can see where each camera is located?

There's some white text at the top of the map that explains exactly what you can use these green glowing things for. These lines are the different vents

throughout the place, and because a vent can either be open or closed, the power is now given to you, the security guard, to decide which ones will be open and which will stay shut. It doesn't seem too important but later on this might be a very useful feature so keep it in mind. These buttons are green when the vents are open but will turn red once you've closed them.

The second of the two buttons out to the left of the map is only sometimes there. It's the "Play Audio" button and it does exactly what you'd think it does. It plays the cutesy little "Hello" sound or the child's laughter that Balloon Boy used to make in the old games. You can choose to make this sound play in every room where there is a security camera but not in any of the ventilation ducts.

What these sounds do is keep SpringTrap in

check. (What's SpringTrap, you ask? Don't worry, we'll get to that.) If you play them in an empty room they'll draw him towards it, so if you want him to stay in one place or in a particular room, play the noise and he'll be stuck in that room for just a little longer. It is the basis for a lot of the strategies to actually beat this game.

The Maintenance Panel: It doesn't need to be said that the new functions of the security camera system are important—you're going to need to use at least some of those functions to survive as a security guard for this new horror attraction. That being said, however, they did bring in all this stuff from the old Freddy Fazbear's Pizza restaurant that are a couple decades old at this point. So the

technology used to put all of this stuff together isn't exactly the most reliable stuff in the world.

Introducing the "Maintenance Panel." Close out of the security camera system on the right of your office and scroll all the way over to the left side. At the bottom of the screen you'll see the small red button you can click to open up this little panel. This thing is going to be incredibly important for keeping all of your advanced security technology working the whole night long.

At some point during the night, probably multiple times, a couple of your systems are going to screw up. That might be the cameras messing up and going all fuzzy or the audio device not working and you end up not being able to draw SpringTrap anywhere. Your vents might even stop working and

the fresh air stops flowing into your office. Any one of these things failing means a lot of trouble for you, so if that ever happens—or maybe even if you think it might be about to happen—you can come over to this panel and reboot any one of the systems individually. Or if they're all broken at the same time then you can choose the "reboot all" option and completely reset all of the systems at once.

The "Maintenance Panel" will play a pivotal role during your stay here so be sure to get comfortable using it.

As a side note, watch out for flashing red lights back in your office—if that's happening then one or more of your systems need to be reset and you've waited for too long. It happens to the ventilation system the most.

FIVE CRAZY NIGHTS

Your Ears: We've said this before, and chances are we're going to say if for every one of the Five Nights at Freddy's games—ou need to listen for specific noises and voices as the night goes on to be prepared for something that's about to happen.

It could be a change in music or you might even start to hear some footsteps like in the earlier games. We can say for a fact that you'll hear some crawling around in the vents again so when you hear anything like that, you need to be ready and react appropriately to the sounds or it could be game over without you even knowing why.

THE CHARACTERS

The characters in this game are another big part of what sets it apart from the other Five Nights at

Freddy's games. Actually it's more so the *lack* of characters that makes this game different.

Would you like to know how many animatronic characters there are going to be running around in the middle of the night coming for you in your slightly larger office? Take a moment to guess—chances are most of you reading this aren't going to get it right.

One. That's right, there's only one animatronic Freddy Fazbear's Pizza character in this game who can actually run through the door to your office and get you. No one's even completely sure who it is anymore—the suit is so old and beat up it's hardly recognizable.

SpringTrap: Its name is SpringTrap, and it's the most decayed looking animatronic you've seen yet. This guy will be wandering through the different

Chapter 3: Five Nights at Freddy's 3

rooms each night as he makes his way towards your office. Most of the things the old animatronic characters did, SpringTrap will also do. This means that not only will you be listening for his footsteps and watching for him through security cameras but he'll also be crawling through the ventilation system as he sneaks around unseen. That vent closing function is starting to make more sense now, isn't it?

He looks a little bit like Bonnie because of his long albeit broken ears, but really SpringTrap is so busted up it's really hard to tell.

His behavior is a little bit trickier to deal with than how the animatronics from the old games acted. You might be able to follow him from room to room but it's going to be really difficult as SpringTrap loves to hide and is particularly good at it.

The Rest of the Characters: We did say that the only character who's really going to come and get you in this game is SpringTrap, and that wasn't a lie. If you ever get a game over it will be because SpringTrap made his way to your office. But there's a weird little thing that happens if the ventilation system stays broken for too long.

When the fresh air stops blowing you're going to start having weird hallucinations. It might be because you're hanging around all this old restaurant stuff or that in reality this haunted house just isn't your cup of tea. Somehow though, all these hallucinations remind you of all of the Freddy Fazbear's Pizza characters of the past that you've been so fond of.

You'll see them on different monitors (don't stare!), and you may even see Freddy himself

walking around just outside the window to your new and improved office. Don't get too scared though, because at the end of the day (or night, in this case), they're just hallucinations and there's nothing really there that can hurt you.

What they can do, however, is make you go crazy. If you manage to see one of these hallucinations on one of the security cameras look away as fast as you can by clicking another camera or just backing out of the system, all the way. Staring at these creepy visions of animatronics from the past start to affect how well these old machines work.

Depending on which character you stare at too long through a security camera, different parts of the security system will be affected negatively. For example, if you see a hallucination of Mangle from Five Nights at Freddy's 2, then your audio system might fail and suddenly you won't be able to hear anything going on in whichever room you're looking into.

We'll go over exactly what each hallucination affects when we start talking strategy, but just know for now that no matter which vision you see, you'll need to look away from it as fast as you can because it will always mean bad news.

FIVE NIGHTS AT FREDDY'S HOUSE OF HORRORS

It might not seem like it but because you really only have to watch out for one animatronic character this time around, for the first time you are going to have the advantage. Because of that, and how

many different places SpringTrap might go and the different ways you can stop him, there's going to be a bunch of different strategies out there you can use to beat this game.

We don't just mean a bunch of different strategies for each night either. In this game you can basically just pick one and use it the whole way through to the fifth night. That doesn't mean it's going to be easy. In fact, it's going to start being a challenge from the second night onwards but for the most part Five Nights at Freddy's 3 is about deciding on your strategy and then getting good enough at it to be able to keep using it as things get harder and faster the further you get.

With all that said, we know there are multiple strategies we could talk about that you could use to beat this game and win. It's just that we really only have so much space in this book to write it all down so what we're going to do is just cover one sure-fire way that will get you through until the end.

Even though we're only going to be covering this one method of beating the game and surviving five nights with SpringTrap prowling around, we will still go over all of the different things you need to be aware of as the night actually progresses. This means that even if you wanted to go off and use another strategy you might have heard of or maybe even one you made up yourself, you can do that and still be confident in your skills because you know what to watch out for.

Now let's get down to the strategy.

Before we start we need go over a few things pertaining to the behavior of SpringTrap. One of the biggest things to remember is that he loves to hide. He can hide in every room there is but when you're looking for him you have to be extra careful because he's very good at being unseen.

The security cameras also do weird things when they're looking at SpringTrap—he has some sort

of effect over them. If you catch him in a room and watch him for too long, the video feed will go all fuzzy. During the time where the screen is all full of static is when SpringTrap actually moves around to another location.

It's also possible to tell when SpringTrap is entering a room you're already looking at. If he's currently not in the room you're seeing through the security camera sometimes the screen will go all fuzzy anyway. It's actually kind of hard to tell because the screen can go fuzzy in this case for two reasons.

1. The screen you're looking at will fill with static when the security camera system needs to be rebooted because of a random hallucination.

2. The screen you're looking at will fill with static for a slightly longer period of time when SpringTrap is moving into it. The challenge will be figuring out what kind of "static" means he just walked in, and what kind of static means you need to reboot the system.

It's learning this behavior and being able to guess where he's going to go that makes getting through Five Nights at Freddy's 3 possible.

Your first night will be a breeze because at this point they haven't brought SpringTrap in so really there's no way for you to lose. The best thing you can do on this night is to get familiar with where all of the cameras are at and figure out how to use the different security systems in place for when you actually will need to use them. We don't really have to worry about using the strategy this night because at this point in the game there's really no one to use it on.

Night two is where the fun begins. If you've been following along you'll know you need to keep all of your systems up and running well, so you know what

to look at and when to reset what system.

If your camera feed is down you reset the camera system. If you can't control the vents you reset the ventilation system. Last but not least, if your audio device system fails you reset it as well. You do this same thing for each of them over at the maintenance panel. If you can get a good handle on all of this, you're really doing good.

The next thing is to try and figure out where SpringTrap hides in every room. The second night is the best for this because he's actually there and he's not as fast or as vicious yet as he could be.

The best way to find him in each room is too look for the whites of his eyes in dark places. There are a few places where you can see his full body but most of the time he'll be in some dark corner where

you cannot see him at all except for his eyes. So get good at spotting them.

Once you've gotten locating him down pat, the next step is to start using the audio device to lure him where you want him to go.

Our strategy this time is to lure him to where you can see him on "Cam 10." If you spot him in that room or in another room that's pretty close to it, use your audio device to play the little kid voice and lure him in there.

Now keep in mind, in almost every room there's a vent connected to the rest of the ventilation system. That is also true for the room we're going to use, so if we don't want him to escape and get to us (which we don't) then the next step (or maybe even the first step—it's up to you) will be to click

the "Map Toggle" button and close the appropriate vent. In this case you check on the vent cameras and double click "Cam 14" to make sure SpringTrap can't get through it.

Once you have all this done, the trick for the rest of the night is to get him to stay where you can see him on "Cam 10." It's fine if he moves away—usually he either tries to go through the vent (which you sealed, so it's fine) or he'll move to another room close by. If that's the case just keep using the audio device to lure him back to "Cam 10."

This seems simple enough, and for the first couple of nights it is. But remember that as each night passes it gets more difficult to keep up with system errors and hallucinations that will prevent you from keeping SpringTrap where you want him

to be. The strategy is simpler in this game but it still takes skill to keep everything working well enough to get done what you need to.

In the later nights it starts to get really bad. Now even if the ventilation system is working fine you're going to get random hallucinations that will mess your game up. Some of the old characters pop up out of nowhere right in your face and can mess any of your other systems up. Don't worry too much though, like we said before, they can't kill you.

Just keep a cool head, reboot what needs rebooting, and make sure you keep luring SpringTrap to where you can see him on "Cam 10" while making sure the vent for "Cam 14" is closed. Do that and you should be able to manage the entirety of Five Nights at Freddy's 3 with relative ease. 🔘

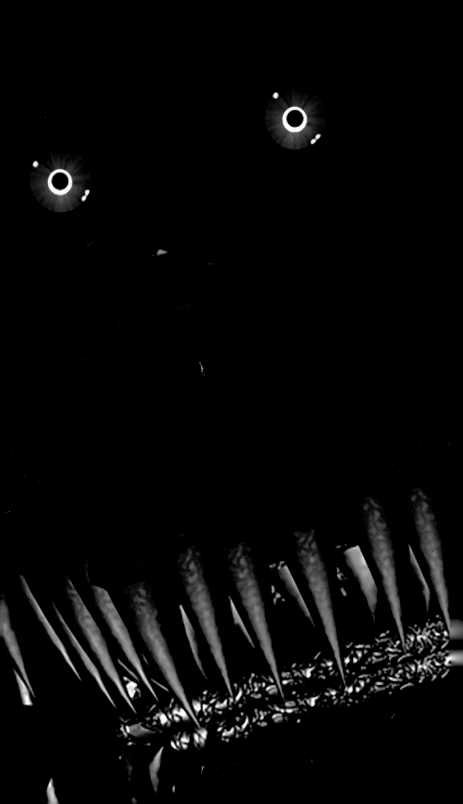

FIVE NIGHTS AT FREDDY'S 4

Welcome to the latest and scariest Five Nights at Freddy's game to date! When we last talked about the third installment there was a lot to say how different it was from the first two games. You had a lot more equipment and there was a big difference in how the game worked.

Prepare to have your mind blown once again as we head into the fourth installment in the Five Nights at Freddy's game series. In each of the past games you had your office, you had security cameras, and you had pizza restaurant scenery all around you.

In this game, all of that is gone. You're no longer a security guard watching over a restaurant at night or an amusement park attraction meant to entertain adults and children alike. In fact, in this particular game you are the kid, and all of those scary animatronics from the Freddy Fazbear's themed places in the past have followed you home to haunt you once again.

The biggest difference? They're all about a thousand percent more terrifying than they were

before and there's only a couple of different ways for you to protect yourself from them. Instead of your fancy office setup with security cameras and monitors to spy on different parts of the building, you've got your two eyes and two ears in a small bedroom.

In terms of what you need to keep track of, there are only two doors to the room you're in, not unlike the office in the original Five Nights at Freddy's. There are doors to your bedroom so you don't have to worry about giving anyone free reign to just walk on in or out whenever they please. But the walls and doors must have been poorly built because unless you're standing at them to hold the doors closed, they're always going to stay open. As each night starts the terrifying new monsters are hiding throughout your house trying to get to you, so the doors are the last line of defense, despite the fact they really don't work like doors should.

There's more to how this game works but we'll go over the rest in just a bit. But first let's go over exactly how you're going to use your flashlight and the different parts in your bedroom that will keep you alive throughout the night.

FIVE CRAZY NIGHTS

YOUR BEDROOM AND WHAT TO USE TO SURVIVE

We'll be honest with you here—there's really not that much you have at your disposal to help keep you alive. There are no more security cameras and no noise makers to lure anyone to another room. There aren't even any light switches on the walls for you to turn on or off.

Thankfully, the light source you do have, your flashlight, is one of those newer models that has battery power to last for days so you really don't have to worry about conserving power in this game. So while it is a short list overall, for the sake of covering all that we need to, we're still going to go over what there is.

Your Feet: Instead of just turning your head slightly to look at one screen or another like in the previous versions of Five Nights at Freddy's, now you're going to turn your character's point of view from looking at the door on one side of the room all the way to the door at the opposite side. There's also a small pit stop you can make to have a look at the closet right in the middle of the room. When you're looking at any of these three doors with your flashlight you can click to have your character run over to them and do one of two things for each: you have the choice to hold the door shut, or peek through the door depending on certain factors which we will go into later.

When you're standing in the middle of the room

normally, however, please note that directly behind you will be your bed, and you're going to need to turn around to look at it more often than not. To do this all you need to do is drag your mouse to the bottom of the screen and click the button to turn around and have a gander at who or what might be chilling out on top of your sheets.

The Doors: Your doors are really your first and last line of defense against any of the nightmares that have followed you home. You have the hallway doors on either side of your room and the closet door in the very middle, and all of them at some point or another can have a horrible monster on the other side of it that you have to keep yourself safe from.

Unfortunately, these doors were all built wrong so they don't work like they should. If no one is there to hold them closed, they'll just hang slightly open. It's not very convenient but for the most part you're only going to have to worry about one at a time. That is, if you're lucky. This rule also applies to the closet door, even though there's not a long hallway on the opposite side of it. This is a decently sized closet and we all know that's where the scariest monsters like to hide.

The other thing you can do—and in some cases, need to do—is to open them wider than they were already and peek through them. If it's the hallway door and you do it right, chances are you're going to see a set of glowing eyes backing down the hallway.

FIVE CRAZY NIGHTS

If you get it wrong, well, it's game over, and at this point you probably know enough about Five Night's at Freddy's to know what game over means.

It works the same for the closet door, and although at the beginning of every night there will be no one inside the closet, that doesn't necessarily remain true for the rest of the night. There might be a couple different monsters who can sneak in and hide there, and part of dealing with them will be either holding the door shut or peeking in occasionally. It might even be a healthy combination of the two.

Your Flashlight: Just like in the previous games, you've got a flashlight to shine in certain areas and even to sometimes stun some monsters to keep them from attacking you. Unlike the other games, however, there's no limit to how long you can use your flashlight. This is probably because it's absolutely impossible to get through even the first night without it. It's nighttime in this kid's house and there are no other lights on so the flashlight is all you have. If you couldn't use it to see, it would be pitch black all night long and impossible to see anything.

Your Ears: This is the last tool on the list and we're wondering if you could hear it coming. Using your ears is a critical part of playing the Five Nights at Freddy's games and in this game using your hearing is more important than it's ever been

Chapter 4: Five Nights at Freddy's 4

before. To make it through the night, you really need to pay more attention to the sounds, voices, and sometimes even the music that plays, announcing the arrival of different nightmares.

There are a bunch of different things that can happen in Five Night's at Freddy's 4 that you'll never know about unless you hear them. Nightmare Chica could be messing around in the kitchen. Nightmare Freddy could sneak right up to your door and unless you're listening carefully for him laughing, you would never know it. So while it's been important in the past games to listen for audio cues and even luring animatronics where you want, it's actually pretty much impossible to win this game without waiting and listening for the right sounds to react to.

CHARACTERS

We're not going to devote a very large section to the characters in this game because if you've been following along in this book and have played all of the previous versions of Five Nights at Freddy's then you've met all of the characters in this game. This is the end of the story for the Five Night's at Freddy's series—you'll most likely see how everything plays out by participating in the mini-games that pop up between each night. But because this is the end to the tale, all the stops are pulled and every single character in the series makes an appearance, but they're not looking the same way you remember them.

FIVE CRAZY NIGHTS

This is a game all about some kid fending off all of the Five Nights at Freddy's characters from his bedroom in the middle of the night with just some doors and a flashlight, so even to start things off it can pretty much be considered a nightmare. What makes things worse, however, is that each and every character from the old games appear in this one as nightmarish versions of themselves. They have glowing and terrifying red eyes, sharp and scary teeth, and all of their faces are warped. There's even nightmare versions of some things you didn't think would count as "characters," like a nightmare cupcake.

We'll list them out here with some quick facts about each.

Nightmare Freddy: Still the same Freddy Fazbear with his hat and bowtie, but stretched out taller with glowing red eyes and a bunch of chunks ripped out of him all over the place. He shows up to the scene with three little mini versions of himself. These three mini versions hang out on your bed and even though it's really easy to check up on them by shining the flashlight, if you don't check up on them enough Nightmare Freddy shows up and gets you.

Nightmare Bonnie: Bonnie's back with sharp teeth, sharp claws, and a big chunk missing

out of his chest so you can see inside. His eyes glow a kind of purple color, unlike Nightmare Freddy, and he comes for you through the left door.

Nightmare Chica: Just every bit as scary as you'd expect from seeing the nightmare versions of the other animatronics. Nightmare Chica is torn and decayed but she's still wearing her bib with "Let's eat!" printed on the front. Nightmare Chica will try to enter through the right door and if you let her sneak inside your room to get behind you, it'll be her cupcake that jumps up to get you seemingly out of nowhere, so watch out.

Nightmare Foxy: Foxy's back for the last time as Nightmare Foxy. He's tall, probably more red than the older version, and just like all the other walking nightmares he's torn up and tattered. He's still got his hook and his teeth are sharper and longer than they ever were before. He doesn't have an eye-patch anymore but he's developed this scary orange glowing eye to make up for it. Nightmare Foxy only starts doing things on the second night and it's possible to see him coming down either hallway alongside Nightmare Bonnie or Nightmare Chica. If you let him sneak inside your room he's going to go right for your closet and stay there. If you leave him

alone in the closet too long he'll eventually come up and get you, so every once in a while you need to check up on him by opening and closing the closet doors until he turns back into a stuffed toy.

PlushTrap: You might guess who this guy's based on if you've played Five Night's at Freddy's 3. PlushTrap is essentially just a stuffed toy version of SpringTrap and you're only going to see him during the mini-game between nights. If you manage to win and beat PlushTrap at this game, it pushes the clock forward by a couple of hours the following night so there's less time you have to wait before the sun comes up at 6:00 am.

Nightmare Fredbear: Ten times scarier than Nightmare Freddy. This guy first shows up on the last night and is there the whole night long instead of Nightmare Freddy. He's bigger, meaner, and both his teeth and claws are sharper and longer. For some reason his hat and bowtie are now pink. When Nightmare Fredbear hits the scene, all of the other animatronic nightmares stay silent because dealing with him is a hassle all in itself. However, since he's just one guy instead of four or five, you might actually have an easier time with him. He'll come at you through the left or right

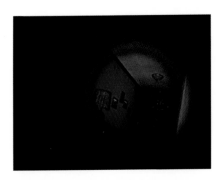

doors, but if you blink a flashlight on and off at him he'll run back down the hall around the corner. Sometimes you might hear him laugh and that could mean a couple different things. It means he's either going to now be in the closet or you'll just see his head sitting by itself on the bed. Shine the light on him if he's on the bed, and just close the door to the closet for a bit if he shows up there.

Nightmare: The final version of Nightmare Fredbear and the most difficult and harsh animatronic nightmare in the game. He really just looks like Nightmare Fredbear but instead of fabric flesh it's just a shadowy mass that separates his insides from the outside. Other than that, his pink tie and top hat are colored yellow now, possibly even scarier than they were before. If you've played the last night in the last couple of games, then you have experience with this sort of thing. We mention this because Nightmare is only going to show up on night seven and in 20/20/20/20 mode in this game.

HOW TO PLAY, SURVIVE, AND WIN

We're going to tell you one strategy that will work for every night for this whole entire game. It's just a simple matter of getting good at it and being able

to click from one thing to the next like a pro.

For this strategy to work, and really for playing this game to win at all, we recommend some sort of stereo sound system. It could be a set of speakers on a laptop, or even some of the cheaper pairs of headphones you can find will do. But you're going to have a really hard time beating this game if you can't hear well. It might even be impossible, really.

You start every night off standing in the middle of the bedroom. The first night you're going to get all the information you need—what you listen for outside the doors and what you need to do based on what you hear. It'll all appear on screen as little instruction text but we'll go over it again here.

You need to get into the habit early on of checking different things all in order and once you've done it, run through and check them all again. It's really up to you what order you check things in but soon enough you won't be deciding anymore. You will just be reacting to the sounds you hear from outside or even inside the bedroom.

To start out, we'll give you an example of what you should be checking out and doing the first couple of nights.

Start by clicking to run over to either door and listening at it. If you hear breathing then you shut the door. If you hear footsteps then you can open

Chapter 4: Five Nights at Freddy's 4

the door and shine the flashlight in whoever's face it happens to be and scare them off. Keep in mind, the left door is Nightmare Bonnie and the right door is Nightmare Chica.

After you're done at the first door to the bedroom, run back and check on the bed. Slowly but surely you will start to see mini Nightmare Freddys pile up on the bed the longer you go without looking at it but shining the flashlight on them makes them go away. You need to keep checking the bed and shining the flashlight on them because if you leave it for too long then Nightmare Freddy himself pops up behind you and it's game over. This rule for checking on the bed will eventually apply to Nightmare Fredbear and Nightmare as well. Instead of seeing the mini Nightmare Freddys you will see just the head of either Nightmare Fredbear or Nightmare and you get rid of them the same way with the flashlight.

After you've checked the bed you can go to the door at the opposite end of the room from where you checked first, and do the same thing. Listen for breathing or footsteps, then do what you need to depending on which one you hear. Either hold the door closed if you hear breathing (when you hear breathing they are right outside the door ready to come in) or open the door and shine the flashlight

at them to make them turn and go the other way. (Turn up the volume so you can hear if the footsteps are getting closer or farther away.)

This is the pattern that needs to repeat for pretty much the entire game. The only difference during each new night is that new characters will be added and you're going to start hearing new and unfamiliar sounds. It could get a little confusing and hard to keep up with after a while.

Sometimes, you might mess up. That's cool, we understand, it's a very scary and nerve wracking game so these things will happen occasionally. What we're going to do though is to give some examples of what might happen when you actually do mess up and how you can keep playing even though you might have missed something.

Normally when you mess up in a Five Nights at Freddy's game, it means game over. Normally. In this game, however, it's possible to screw up and still last until 6:00 am.

Sometimes you might hear footsteps coming towards a door and you're at the wrong place at the wrong time. If you're at the door on the right and someone's about to come in on the left, chances are you won't make it across the room in time. Usually this spells disaster unless the one who happened to be at the door is Foxy. Which it usually is.

FIVE CRAZY NIGHTS

If Nightmare Foxy or Nightmare Freddy manage to sneak in the room while you're distracted by something else, they usually make a run for the closet and hide in it. They won't be the only ones that do this either but we're just going to talk about them because they do the same thing everyone else does in the closet.

Once they're in there, they won't come up until morning so you're stuck with them. The thing is, that doesn't mean you're going to lose. What actually changes is that you now have to add an extra step to the strategy of checking the doors and the bed. If you leave Nightmare Foxy or Nightmare Freddy in the closet for too long, eventually they jump out at you and that's game over. To avoid this, you need to start checking up on them every so often and closing the closet door on their faces a couple times.

After the closet door has been closed on them a few times they will revert back to just a normal stuffed toy version of themselves and they won't cause harm to you for a bit. Keep in mind it's not permanent—eventually they're going to be big scary nightmares again and you have to do the closet thing all over again. But if you can, you can win out through the night and they'll be out of your closet

when the next night starts.

We don't have the space to go over the behavior of every nightmare character but this strategy will work for all the characters and each new night.

To sum up it looks like this:

· Check for breathing or footsteps at the first bedroom door and respond appropriately (flashlight if footsteps, close door if breathing).

· Go to opposite bedroom door and repeat the steps for the first door.
· Check on the bed for mini Freddys (or Nightmare Fredbear head) and shine light on them so they go away.

· Always listen for footsteps or other signal noises in case something happens when you're not at a door. Depending on what noise you hear, respond appropriately.

· If you make a mistake and someone gets in, just hope that it's Nightmare Foxy or Nightmare Freddy and start to regularly check the closet door as well (shut the closet door on whoever is inside and they will eventually turn into a small

stuffed toy).

If you practice this strategy enough, it will eventually get to a point where you could even consider this game to be easy. The steps you take over and over again will carry you all the way to the final night without any problems if you get good enough at clicking back and forth.

Definitely make sure you can hear everything you need to hear right from the start. There's no security cameras in this game, so the only real way to tell where anyone is or what they're doing is by listening to the noises they make.

Power through with this strategy until even the eighth night to finally unravel the mystery behind all of these Five Nights at Freddy's games and maybe even get a small peek at what's coming up at a later date! ⬤

FREDDY'S HISTORY AND CREATOR BIO

Horror games have been around as long as video games have existed, even predating the Atari 2600. The first instances of survival horror can be traced back to 1992. Alone in the Dark for DOS was the first 3D survival-horror game, and Night Trap for the SegaCD was the first to combine live-action footage and a point-and-click interface.

Since its release in 2014, Five Nights at Freddy's has been one of the most popular independent survival games around. Within two years, the game has spawned three sequels, with the fifth installment, "Sister Location," to be released in the fall of 2016. There is also a movie on the horizon, a novel to be released in 2016, and the game is in the process of moving from mobile and PC into the console markets.

Five Nights at Freddy's instantly became known for its tense gameplay, creepy ambience, and mysterious backstory, making it both a fun and exciting game, and an instant hit with YouTube gamers, racking up millions of views and becoming a huge seller on the Steam, IOS, and Android platforms. Your goal is to survive all five nights, a task that becomes harder and harder each night. Events come faster and faster, and the tension mounts, creating a one-of-a-kind gaming experience that has brought gamers back again and again.

FNF's creator, independent game developer and animator Scott Cawthon, says the concept behind the game was equal parts accident and inspiration.

"I'd made a family friendly game about a beaver before this, but when I tried to put it online it got torn apart by a few prominent reviewers. People said that the main character looked like a scary animatronic animal. I was heartbroken and was ready to give up on game-making. Then one night something just snapped in me, and I thought to myself—I bet I can make something a lot scarier than that," Cawthorn told Indiegamemag.com in 2014.

FIVE CRAZY NIGHTS

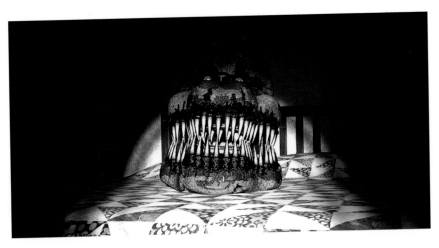

Cawthon, a Texas native, first came on the scene in 2007 with a series of animated YouTube videos, and several independent games such as The Pilgrim's Progress, Chipper and Sons Lumber Company, and The Desolate Hope. At the time, these games found limited success. Even though the Five Nights at Freddy's franchise has been universally praised and received huge acclaim, Cawthon is careful to still be the person he has always been. "I spend my evenings playing Megaman 3, Buster only, with my kids. And I try to (do) good with what's been given to me," he told Toucharcade.com in 2015.

By 2015, the game had received several awards, countless positive reviews, and the film rights had been sold to Warner Brothers. Once Five Nights at Freddy's took off on multiple platforms, a sequel was soon in the works. Three months later, in November of 2014, Five Nights at Freddy's 2 was released on Steam. In January of 2014, Five Nights at Freddy's 2 won two FEAR awards—Best Indie and Game of the Year. Five Nights at Freddy's also won for Most Original game.

With two solid hits under his belt, Cawthon moved ahead with the release of Five Nights at Freddy's 3 in March of 2015, expanding the backstory using hints, Easter eggs, and vague messages that had gamers playing over and over, looking for clues to the history.

Cawthon, while very in touch with and considerate of his fan base, does enjoy using mysterious messages on his website as teasers for upcoming releases, and has even gone so far as to pull a prank on the

Chapter 5: Freddy's History and Creator Bio

game's fans. While developing Five Nights at Freddy's 3, he released a fake message stating that he had been hacked and that the new game was cancelled, even going so far as to provide a link for a fake game that was intentionally bad.

By the summer of 2015, it was time for a new chapter in the series, and Five Nights at Freddy's 4 was released that July. The latest chapter proved to be a departure from the previous games, and added another twist to the history behind the games. In October of 2015, Cawthon released bonus content for part 4, a Halloween edition that replaced the nightmare creatures with Halloween versions.

Its popularity with fans has led to endless web pages dedicated to figuring out the mysteries that lie at the core of the game's storyline, although, according to Cawthon, nobody has gotten all of it right as of yet.

In August of 2015, he told Forbes, "You know, when I released the first game over a year ago, I was amazed at how quickly everyone found every bit of lore and story. Then the same happened with part 2, fans and YouTubers dug in and found everything. Game Theory did an incredible video on part 2; getting almost everything right. Then part 3 came out, and once again the story was uncovered by the community. It seemed that there was nothing I could hide! But then I released part 4, and somehow.... no one, not a single person, found the pieces. The story remains completely hidden. I guess most people assumed that I

DID YOU KNOW?

Scott Cawthon is the voice of the Phone guy in the first three games. He is also the only employee at Scott Games, handling every part of the game development process himself.

FIVE CRAZY NIGHTS

filled the game with random Easter eggs this time. I didn't. What's in the box? It's the pieces put together. But the bigger question is, would the community accept it that way? The fact that the pieces have remained elusive this time strikes me as incredible, and special, a fitting conclusion in some ways, and because of that, I've decided that maybe some things are best left forgotten, forever."

In January of 2016, Cawthon took the franchise in a different direction with the release of Five Nights at Freddy's World, an RPG based on the horror hit. Responding to the fans, and wanting to improve the game's quality, he quickly pulled the game, revamped many elements of the gameplay, and re-released it on Steam a couple of months later for free.

No matter what the future holds for the franchise, Cawthon hopes that kids find inspiration in his independent games, and that they, in turn, will become the next generation of game creators.

"I'm getting too old for this. And when I retire someday, I'm going to want to sit down at a computer and play YOUR games, read YOUR stories, and watch YOUR videos. Don't fall in with the people who have already given up on themselves. You are tomorrow's next big thing," he told Touchacarde.com in July 2015. Luckily, with so many projects on the horizon, it doesn't seem like Cawthon will be retiring any time soon.

But what is it about the Five Nights at Freddy's franchise that has made it so wildly popular? Some people believe that it may be

a fear of animatronics and pizza places. Others have pointed to the gameplay itself, and the fact that not being able to move creates a sense of helplessness.

To understand the game's popularity, we have to look at what makes being scared a fun thing. The key to its success lies in the game capitalizing on one thing—the art of the "jump scare". A jump scare is the reaction you have when something surprises you, or pops up unexpectedly, and is the basis for many scary movies, TV shows, video games, and haunted house attractions.

Over the last five years, live streaming has become a big business in the gaming world, and watching your favorite YouTuber get scared makes you want to buy the game and have the same experience. The jump scares in Five Nights at Freddy's are extra effective because there is always the chance you might survive, but at the same time, you know they are coming for you, and you still have to quickly perform multiple tasks. The most important device for this in the game is the need to monitor the remote camera system. You HAVE to look away from the room you are in, and when you come back....that's when they get you.

Two years after its original release, and with much more on the way in the near future, the Five Nights at Freddy's franchise is stronger than ever. Fans are excited to see what is going to come next, and if Scott Cawthon stays true to form, there should be plenty more scares to share. ⊗

DID YOU KNOW?
The original release date for part 4 was October 31, 2015, but Cawthon moved the date back to August, and then wound up releasing the game on July 23.

THE UNLUCKY
13 SURVIVAL HORROR GAMES

Although the Five Nights at Freddy's series has brought back the jump scare in a big way, it's not the first game to use this technique to excite and terrify gamers. Here's a list of 13 survival horror games that will make it hard to sleep at night. **Play if you dare!**

RESIDENT EVIL

The father of the modern-day survival horror game, Resident Evil burst onto the scene in 1996 on the original Playstation. Combining third-person combat, puzzle solving, and a mysterious zombie outbreak in Raccoon City, the game became an instant classic, spawning numerous sequels, a film franchise, and forever changing horror games. Resident Evil was the first game that truly brought the zombie experience to the player, and has been copied countless times in the 20 years since its release. Its immediate sequels, Resident Evil 2 and Resident Evil Nemesis, expanded on the original's success with better gameplay and even more scares, setting a standard for all the games that were to follow. Most fans agree that the series peaked with the release of Resident Evil 4 in 2005. Resident Evil 7 was announced in June of 2016.

SILENT HILL

The next heavy hitter in the survival horror genre was 1999's Silent Hill. The game takes place in the abandoned, foggy town of Silent Hill, and uses its misty environment and brilliant sound design to play with your mind and create fear. Things really start to ramp up when reality switches over to the "Otherworld," a living nightmare where terrifying creatures come to life, and you receive strange visions that further reveal the story. As the game unfolds, things only get worse from there. The huge success of Silent Hill resulted in 11 video game sequels, a comic book series, multiple novels, and two film adaptations.

CLOCK TOWER

A mid-1990s classic that was eventually remade for Playstation and Windows, Clock Tower is a very cool, spooky, 3D point-and-click horror game, where you play as a young girl who has to solve the mysteries of Barrow Mansion while avoiding the deadly scissors of nine-year-old Bobby Barrow. The game relies heavily on exploration, solving puzzles, and the ever-present danger of your child stalker to create tension, and featured multiple endings determined by your actions during the game. Clock Tower developed a loyal international fan base which led to two sequels for the Playstation 2, 2002's Clock Tower 3 and 2005's Haunting Grounds.

ALIEN ISOLATION

One of the scariest, most tense games in recent memory is 2014's Alien Isolation for the current console generation. The game uses sneaking, hiding, and a relentless, unstoppable alien to drive the fear level through the roof. Making matters worse are the human survivors, and the lengths they will go to in order to stay alive. Any sound you make attracts the alien, and there are few things more primal than hiding in a locker, holding your breath, while the alien sniffs for you a few inches from your face. Travelling back and forth across the hostile space station takes nerves of steel and incredible patience. Alien Isolation is the ultimate in sci-fi survival horror.

ALONE IN THE DARK: THE NEW NIGHTMARE

Released in 2001 for PC and the Playstation 2, Alone in the Dark: The New Nightmare took elements from earlier installments and combined them with a Resident Evil styled control system and overall feel. The game takes place on Shadow Island and has you searching for three ancient tablets, and attempting to solve the mysterious death of your friend. Quickly, you find out that the island is a portal to the World of Darkness and all sorts of monsters are out to get you. Many objects are hidden in the dark, so finding items with your flashlight is a huge part of the puzzle solving. A classic, creepy mansion game.

DEAD ISLAND

If hordes of classic zombies taking over a resort on a tropical island sounds like a good time, the 2011 first-person combat crafter Dead Island might be a fun way to get in some quality beach horror time. A large, open world and a wide variety of weapon mods make this game stand out from the large amount of zombie games available in the last five years. Plenty of side quests, lots of scavenging, and limited ammunition will have you developing strategies to survive so you can get off the island.

DOOM 3

In a departure from the groundbreaking first-person-shooter action of Doom and Doom2, Doom 3 introduced an extremely dark, effective horror feel with its 2004 debut. Taking full advantage of the cramped conditions inside Mars City, a space outpost, Doom 3 is one of the first games to hit you with jump scares through the entire game, making for an incredibly tense thrill ride. As you move through the game, the terror piles up and you begin to fear every shadow and every turn in the endless maze of corridors. Play this in the dark if you dare.

DEAD SPACE

Influenced heavily by Doom 3, Dead Space introduced us to its creepy space mining ship in 2008, along with a ton of jump scares and the urgent need to remove the arms and legs of the savage Necromorphs that have taken over. Using a perfect blend of tight spaces, dark corners, sound effects, and a haunting musical score, Dead Space hits you over and over again in all of your scared places. The game's success has resulted in two game sequels and a mobile version, as well as an animated film, comic books, novels, and a film deal.

AMNESIA: THE DARK DESCENT

In classic survival horror style, Amnesia: The Dark Descent takes away the thing we need the most in horrifying situations: the ability to fight back. This 2010 scare-fest has you running around a creepy castle, avoiding the monsters that dwell within. In order to stay sane, you cannot stay in the dark for too long, but light sources make you more visible to the monsters. If you are spotted, your only choice is to run and hide. Being trapped in a room while a monster bangs on the door will bring your fear to a whole new level. A sequel, Amnesia: A Machine for Pigs, was released in 2013.

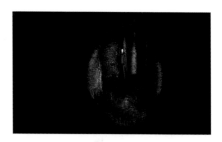

THE EVIL DEAD: HAIL TO THE KING

One of the first successful adaptations of a horror movie franchise, 2000's The Evil Dead: Hail to the King perfectly captures the feeling of the isolated cabin and the ominous forest from the Evil Dead films. Striking a balance of scary and humorous, running around with a shotgun and a chainsaw has never been so much fun. Explore the fruit cellar, uncover secret tunnels, and wander the narrow forest paths, fighting hordes of Deadites, skeletons, Hellbillies, and Wolverine Scouts along the way.

SLENDER: THE EIGHT PAGES

Based on the urban legend of Slender Man, Parsec Productions released the very creepy Slender: The Eight Pages in 2012. The game takes place in a dark forest where you have to collect eight pages scattered amongst the trees and empty buildings. The more pages you collect, the thicker the fog becomes, and the more often Slender appears, just beyond your vision. The pounding of drums in the distance makes it hard to avoid running, but whatever you do, do not look behind you. The game's success led to a sequel, Slender: The Arrival, which was released in 2013.

OUTLAST

This 2013 release is one of the premier examples of modern survival horror. Outlast combines the classic "run and hide" gameplay with beautiful next-gen graphics, creepy atmosphere, and plenty of jump scares. You play as Miles Upshur, a journalist investigating strange events at Mount Massive Asylum. The key game mechanics in Outlast are the use of a video camera with night vision to see in dark areas, and first-person gameplay that gives Outlast a "found footage" feel. Outlast: Whistleblower DLC was released in the spring of 2014, and a sequel is scheduled to be released before the end of 2016.

THE LAST OF US

The crowning achievement of the last generation of consoles, and one of the finest narrative video games of all time, very few gaming experiences come close to 2013's The Last of Us. You play as Joel, an unwilling hero who has to escort a young girl, Ellie, across a post-apocalyptic United States, surviving against marauding gangs, crazy survivalists, and infected zombies. A deep story, an environment-influenced combat system with stealth elements, and tense monster interactions will have you on the edge of your seat from Boston to Salt Lake City. After winning numerous Game of the Year awards, the game's developer, Naughty Dog, has announced that a sequel is in the works.

HOW TO ILLUSTRATE SCARINESS

Drawing scary creatures can sometimes be as rewarding as fighting them or running away from them in a video game. The creation of illustrations is a huge part of video games, both to create an artistic vision as well as to create what you actually see on the screen. Artwork can also be used to enhance books, and to make entire cartoons and animated movies. Some films use traditional drawings, some use stop-motion figures, and others use computer programs, but the techniques for character creation remain the same.

All of the tools and skills used to draw people and animals can also be used to make these characters scary. Recent films such as *ParaNorman* and the *Hotel Transylvania* movies have found lots of success using equal amounts of cute and creepy to tell their stories. By learning a few basic techniques, you can turn any type of drawing into a scary creation, and come up with your own creepy creatures to terrify your friends and family.

WHAT MAKES A DRAWING SCARY?

There are many different ways to make an illustration scary, and it will always come back to figuring out what makes you scared. Drawing a figure in a menacing posture or giving a creature or person an angry face can be a good place to start. Slanted eyebrows can change a face dramatically. Changing parts of a person's physical structure also works really well. Making the eyeballs one solid color, stretching the face, and giving your character really long fingers are just a few examples of small changes to what we consider "normal" that can make a person or animal look scary.

Removing every day things also works really well. A famous example would be Slender Man. The main reason he is scary is because the artist made him without a face. Another thing to consider is the size of the scary subject. A creature can be cute and fun when it's tiny, but make it the size of your bed, and all of a sudden, it's not nearly as cute anymore. Another example would be the animatronics in Five Nights at Freddy's. Large animals that sing and move around can be lots of fun during the daytime,

but if you are alone with them at night, it can be really spooky. Play around with making arms and legs longer than usual. Little changes can go a long way towards turning regular objects into things you wouldn't want to bump into at night.

Just like when writing a story, the location of your subject and the environment can have a huge effect on how scary a picture is. Imagine a drawing of a stuffed rabbit. Not so scary, right? But take that same rabbit, and put it in a graveyard at night,

or make it come out of your dark closet while you are sleeping, or put it in the middle of your lawn on Halloween night...all of a sudden, it's not as cute and cuddly as it was just a moment ago.

The more you practice, the better you will get at both drawing and making your drawings spooky. Always keep pushing yourself to try drawing new things and using new materials, but remember: the most important tool in your toolbox is your imagination. Experiment and have fun!

ANIMATED BEAR

1: Start by drawing two circles and an oval. Finding the basic shape of your art subject is the first thing you should do. Circles, ovals, and cylinders work great to make bodies, heads, arms, and legs on living creatures like animals and people.

2: Draw circles for the ears, eyes, snout, and stomach. Draw shapes for the arms and legs. You can see your drawing begin to take form as you add more shapes to your basic figure. Even at this early stage, you can already tell what it's going to be. Notice how the placement of our basic shapes creates a pose that gives a sense of motion.

3: Add more circles for the ears, eyes, mouth, nose, hands, and feet. As we add more shapes, the details begin to come to life....hopefully this bear doesn't!

4: Add eyebrows, and draw lines connecting each part together. Draw two ovals in the left hand. What do the eyebrows tell you about the bear's mood? Right now, he looks angry, but change the angle and he can look surprised or happy. Also keep in mind that a happy face can be scary if the environment is spooky!

5: Draw circles on the cheeks and a bandage on the body. Small details like the bandage add depth to our character's story. Draw the top of the hat, and lines for the toes. Give our friend fingers on his right hand by adding four ovals.

6: Draw eyes. Add extra lines to the hat, arms, and neck. It's these final details that bring the drawing together, and make our bear seem much more real. You now have your own animatronic bear to entertain during the day and terrorize at night!

1: Start by drawing a circle, an oval, and a square body. Our cat will have a similar setup to our dog character.

2: Draw triangles for the ears, almond shapes for the eyes, a peanut shape for the snout, and four ovals for the feet. Add a half circle below the snout for the cat's mouth. You can give him a slightly different expression by rotating the eyes slightly.

3: Add triangles to the ears, lines to the eyes, a shape for the nose, and ovals for the mouth and front legs. Draw notches at the cheeks to simulate fluffy fur.

4: Draw lines connecting the ears to the head, and the head to the body. Draw half circles for the back legs and to mark the paws. Add a tail. I really hope he is an outside cat.

5: Add lines for the toes, the tip of the tail, and to mark the brow. Draw circles for the teeth. The round teeth give the impression that the mouth is open.

6: Add eyebrows, eyes, and whiskers. I sure can't wait to see him at the foot of the bed in the middle of the night! Here kitty, kitty!

GIANT SPIDER

1: Start by drawing two curved lines for the spider. Draw an oval and five curved lines for the runner. Even at this early stage, you can get a sense of action in our character.

2: Draw an oval for the runner's eye, and add lines to shape the rest of him. Draw two ovals to start the spider's mouth. Begin drawing long lines to create the spider's legs. Notice how the drawing is even scarier because the spider is so big.

3: Add two more ovals to make the runner's other eye and mouth. Draw pointed teeth for the spider's mouth and add circles for its eyes. Draw curved lines to create the spider's claws and lower body. When you draw the claws above and below the runner, it adds a feeling of danger.

4: Add hair to the runner and add lines to mark his thumb. Draw a jagged line to finish the spider's mouth. Add more curved lines to complete the spider's claws. Extra teeth tend to make a monster scarier.

5: Draw lines to mark the runner's clothes and add an oval to create his tongue. Begin to draw more lines behind the spider as you decide where to place his legs. Not only do the legs on the far side of the spider enhance the sense of movement, they also add a three-dimensional quality to the drawing.

6: Add two circles for the runner's eyes. Stripes or other patterns can be placed on the spider's back. Good job! You've made your own giant spider...now start running!

1: Start by drawing a circle, an oval, and a square body with rounded shoulders. Just like with our bear character, the basic shapes set up what the drawing is doing.

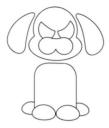

2: Draw teardrop shapes for the ears, half circles for the eyes, a peanut shape for the snout, and four ovals for the feet. Instead of using eyebrows, this time we will change the basic eye shape to look angry.

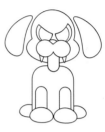

3: Add lines for the eyes and nose, triangles for the teeth, and ovals for the tongue and front legs. I don't think this dog wants to play!

4: Draw lines connecting the ears to the head, and the head to the body. Draw half circles for the back legs and to mark the paws. Notice how you have created a collar with the neck lines. Adding spikes is optional.

5: Add lines for the toes and to mark the brow. Draw a center line for the tongue. Just a few more details, and he will be ready to bury some bones in the backyard.

6: Final details include circles for the eyes, and a small crease at the bottom of the snout. Take him for a walk and introduce him to all your friends!

HOW TO WRITE A SCARY STORY

Everybody loves a good story, and because of that, there are many different types of fiction that appeal to the many types of people in the world. Epic adventures, fairy tales, comedy, and serious dramas are just a few of the styles used to tell different types of stories.

If you look at your favorite book, movie, or video game, the one thing they all have in common is that they present characters and situations that draw you in, take you on a journey, and make you want to know how the story ends. Writing stories of your own is a fun way to use your imagination to bring characters and places to life. But what if you wanted to write a scary story? And what is it, exactly, that makes a story scary?

What Scares YOU?

In order to make a scary story, the first thing you have to do is answer a question—what scares YOU? Some people are scared of the dark, or monsters, or clowns, or spiders. The best stories come from your own experiences, and the scariest stories will always come from the things that scare you.

Another thing to consider is if whatever it is that scares you is scary to other people as well. You might be completely terrified of puppies, but that may not be true for other people. When something can scare you as well as others, it's called a "common fear." Using a common fear in your story will make it scary for more people, and the more people that get scared by it, the better the story is.

A smart way to begin is to make a list of all of the scary things you can think of, and then pick one to begin with. Making lists is a great way to keep track of your ideas for future stories.

Scary Places, Scary Times

Another way you can find your common fear is to use places that people consider scary. Old, empty houses are almost always haunted. Nobody wants to walk through a graveyard at night. What happens at the circus after the lights go out? All of these are great places to start, but if you use your imagination, you can make a scary place out of almost anywhere. Most people have been afraid of the dark at some time in their lives, so nighttime will always create a spooky mood. Everyone knows that if you're not careful, bad things can happen at midnight. Events like Halloween and other holidays can also make a nice beginning for your story.

Nature Can Be Scary, Too

What mysteries are hiding within the fog? Do thunder and lightning make you want to get under the covers? Why do forests sound spooky at night? What might live in that cave? Are those voices in the wind? Nature is a fantastic way to give your story depth and can provide plenty of creepy settings. Deep water, snowy wilderness, never-ending forest, craggy mountains, murky swamps—the natural world can be a frightening place, especially after the sun goes down.

Starting Your Story

Before you can get to any of the scary stuff, a writer needs to set up some basic story elements. Who is the main character? Where does the story take place? What situation is the character in? Once the audience has this information, you can bring in the scary part. If you pretend that you are the person in the story, you can also get a sense of what could be scary.

For example, if we take a boy named Billy, put him in his house, in his bedroom, and we make it nighttime, we have set up a quick, easy way to introduce our common fear. Is there a sound outside his window? Or in his closet? Or under his bed? Is there a stuffed animal looking at him? By setting up a scene—a boy alone in his room at night—we have everything we need to make the story scary.

But why is it that a boy named Billy in his room at night is a scary thing? It's a very simple answer, and it's the main reason that a story is able to be scary. The reason is because we have ALL been alone in our room at night, so we understand what he is going through. Since we have all shared this feeling, as an audience we start to care what happens to

the boy. We share his experience, so when he gets scared, WE get scared. When Billy makes a decision, we agree or disagree. When the reader cares, they have no choice but to go on the journey you are creating, and that is the magic of storytelling.

Every Story Has Three Parts

Now that we have a character, a place, and a common fear picked out, what comes next? If you look at most stories, they usually have a beginning, a middle, and an end. The beginning is the introduction we already talked about. We tell the reader who the character is, where they are at, and what they are doing.

The beginning section will also be where we bring in our common fear. Once we have that in place, we can move to the middle. This is where young Billy would make a choice. Will he investigate the sound? Will he hide under his blankets? Will he run out of his room? Whatever choices Billy makes will lead to the ending.

After we have our intro and our middle, we can write our ending. Think of the ending as an answer to a question. We meet Billy, Billy is scared...is there a reason for Billy to be scared or was it Billy's imagination? That answer is the ending of our story. When you need to ask story questions, answer them as you would in real life. If you were Billy, would you investigate the sound?

Normal Things Can Be Spooky, Too

Another fun way to use your imagination while writing a story is to see if you can take a normal household object and make it scary. What if a monster lived in your TV? What if your furniture

moved around at night?

Using everyday objects that everybody has in their homes is a great way to create a common fear. You can also create common fears from other things that aren't normally scary to you. The person who delivers your mail, the school you go to, a birthday present, a favorite toy—any of those can be super scary if you put them in the right situation.

Putting It All Together

Now we can put all of these ideas to work for us. First, you will need an outline. An outline is a type of list that contains all of your story ideas and makes it easier to remember important characters and events.

Keep your outline simple using the "Story Has Three Parts" rules. Separate the beginning, middle, and ending and put your character and location at the start. This is also where you would put weather conditions, time of day, or a holiday. Place your common fear between the beginning and the middle.

Next, write down any scary things that are going to happen to the character and the questions that the character has to ask himself. Place the answers to the questions between the middle and end sections. Then, just write what happens to the character at the end. Once you have all of these things in your outline, writing the story will be much easier.

After you're done, read it a few times and see if it needs any changes. Letting family and friends read your story is also a great way to get ideas on how to make it better.

The fun part about writing scary fiction is that the answers to story questions help you learn about yourself. What is scary to you? What would you do in a dark forest with the wind howling on Halloween night? Would you be brave or would you run?

With a little practice, you'll find that it's easy to turn any story into a scary story, so put that imagination to work, and maybe you will be the one who writes the next great scary video game, spooky movie, or creepy book. 🕱